Working from Home

Working from Home

Earn a Living Where You Live

Jane Jerrard ▶

an imprint of the American Library Association

HURON STREET ⏚ PRESS

CHICAGO • 2013

© 2013 by the American Library Association. Any claim of copyright is subject to applicable limitations and exceptions, such as rights of fair use and library copying pursuant to Sections 107 and 108 of the U.S. Copyright Act. No copyright is claimed for content in the public domain, such as works of the U.S. government.

Printed in the United States of America
17 16 15 14 13   5 4 3 2 1

Extensive effort has gone into ensuring the reliability of the information in this book; however, the publisher makes no warranty, express or implied, with respect to the material contained herein.

ISBNs: 978-1-937589-11-0 (paper); 978-1-937589-05-9 (PDF); 978-1-937589-27-1 (ePub); 978-1-937589-28-8 (Kindle). For more information on digital formats, visit the ALA Store at alastore.ala.org and select eEditions.

Library of Congress Cataloging-in-Publication Data
Jerrard, Jane.
  Working from home : earn a living where you live / Jane Jerrard.
     p.   cm.
  Includes bibliographical references and index.
  ISBN 978-1-937589-11-0 (alk. paper)
  1. Telecommuting. 2. Home-based businesses. I. Title.
  HD2336.3.J47 2013
  658'.0412—dc23
                                                                                2012023896

Series book design in Liberation Serif, Union, and Soho Gothic by Casey Bayer
Cover image © Iriana Shiyan/Shutterstock, Inc.

♾ This paper meets the requirements of ANSI/NISO Z39.48-1992 (Permanence of Paper).

Contents

Preface

Many of today's workers (and would-be workers) idealize the work-from-home lifestyle. Different people are drawn to different aspects of home-based work—it could be trading in a daily commute for a more flexible lifestyle with more personal time; the independence of working alone; or the comfort of leaving your business casual outfit in the closet and working in your pajamas.

But the reality is that working from home is not all free time and cozy flannel. There are always downsides, and this way of living is definitely not for everyone. For one thing, working from home is likely to mean *more* time on the job than working in an employer's office; the increased productivity that is generally seen in telecommuting employees comes from more hours spent on the job.

Whether you would simply prefer to work from home or your circumstances leave no other option for making money, getting started on your goal is the toughest part. That's why we devote space in this book to helping readers figure out what types of work to seek and how to find it. We cover both here in detail and recommend specific resources. You also get a realistic look at what it is like to work from home, as well as suggestions for practical steps you can take to ensure success in your home-based job.

Much of this advice is necessarily general, because it is meant to apply to any work that can be done from home, from data entry to dog walking to DJing to digital consulting. We cover part-time work, freelance work, and businesses "on the side" as well as full-time career employment.

After reviewing the basics of all home-based employment in part I, we divide the rest of the book into two additional sections. Part II addresses telecommuting—working from home for an employer. Part III is about starting and running your own home-based business—including some fundamentals to consider.

Whether you are eager to exchange your cubicle for your kitchen table or want to follow your passion by starting your own business, this book offers unique guidance, ideas, and insights that should get you started on your path toward reaching your goal, which happens to be at home.

Part I

Working from Home

ONE

The Basics of Working from Home

If your goal is to make money without leaving the comfort of your own home, you're living in the right time. Today more than ever, employers are more apt to allow their workers to telecommute. After all, it's more cost-effective for companies to hire staff who work off-site than to support an office. At the same time, more entrepreneurial spirits are starting their own businesses from their homes.

So the odds of realizing your goal are in your favor—and you can improve those odds by preparing yourself with some solid information. This chapter and the next lay the groundwork for those seriously considering working from home, providing an overview of telecommuting and self-employment.

A Popular Trend

It is difficult to find specific data on how many people work from home, because many statistics include employees who are allowed to work occasionally or regularly from home but are primarily located at their workplace. However, in the 2008 U.S. Census 5.9 million people said their home was "their principal place of work." That number included 3.1 million who ran their own business, so at that time some 2.8 million employees—or just over 2 percent of the employed population—worked at home for their employer.

This percentage is even larger if you consider those who occasionally work from home. According to WorldatWork, a nonprofit organization that monitors human resources issues, in 2010 a whopping 26.2 million employees worked from home (or remotely) at least one day a month. That's 20 percent of the entire U.S. workforce. As for people who run their own businesses from home, that number varies as well, but it could be as high as 38 million, according to U.S. Census statistics.

In a 2008 survey by staffing company Robert Half International, a whopping 72 percent of employees indicated that flexible work arrangements would cause them to choose one job over another. Thirty-seven percent specifically named telecommuting.

> "There are many good things about working from home. What I like most is that it's quiet and I can concentrate much better than I can at the office surrounded by my cube mates. A close second is that I get to sleep almost two hours longer than I would if I were traveling to the office. More reasons: I don't get caught up in office politics or office frenzy. I get to run a load of laundry while I'm working and take my dogs out during the day so they don't have to 'hold it' for twelve hours. I can make doctor's appointments and other personal calls without everyone knowing my business. And I don't get colds very often, because no one is coughing on me."
>
> —*Diana Wellington, marketing manager*

Employers are now more accepting and even enthusiastic about their workers getting jobs done remotely. WorldatWork's 2008 survey of 2,288 U.S. companies showed that 42 percent of respondents allowed employees to work remotely—a huge increase from just 30 percent the year before.

Telecommuting Savings

There are multiple benefits and savings associated with hiring workers remotely, according to Herb Cogliano, CEO of national IT contract staffing company Sullivan & Cogliano. "Companies have access to less expensive labor pools," he points out. "This doesn't mean just offshore, but if you're based in Boston, or L.A., or New York, you can hire a phenomenal worker who lives in, say, North Dakota, and pay a lower rate than you would for someone in your major metropolitan market."

Even the U.S. government values the cost savings of having employees supply their own workspace—and the increased productivity that results. For example, at the U.S. Patent and Trademark Office more than half of the approximately 10,000 employees work remotely full-time, and the rest do so part-time. Internal audits show that those patent examiners who work remotely put in an average of 14 hours more work each year than their office-bound counterparts. And the agency estimates that it saves nearly $20 million in office space costs.[1]

The Telework Research Network estimates the following benefits to organizations that employ telecommuters:

Productivity increase: 27%

Reduction in real estate: 18%

Reduction in office building electricity: 18% (net of home office electricity)

Reduction in unscheduled absences: 63%

Reduction in employee attrition: 25%

Who's the Boss?

For some, the idea of working from home involves reporting in to a corporate headquarters from your home office; for others, it's starting up a small business in the basement. These types of home-based jobs are radically different—and covered separately in the two parts of this book.

There is another, hybrid kind of working from home: working as a long-term contractor or temp worker through an agency. In this scenario, your agency may find you the work and will definitely send you a steady paycheck (and even take out standard payroll taxes) for the duration. Your contract with an organization may run weeks, months, or even years. However, there is no guarantee that the work will continue endlessly; working as an independent contractor is a lot like being self-employed in many regards. Writer Heather Z. Hutchins was surprised to discover that many people work as long-term contractors from home and have been doing it for years. "I didn't know that this type of job even existed. If I had known, I might have done this earlier. I liked my time as a freelancer, but it was a feast or famine kind of work environment. Now, I have a steady workflow *and* a steady paycheck."

Choosing Work You Can Do at Home

So many jobs are routinely filled by employees working from their homes—and even more when you count people who run their own home-based businesses. According to *Occupational Outlook Quarterly,* the most logical telecommuting tasks are those that "require concentration and large blocks of uninterrupted, independent time . . . have well defined beginning and end points . . . [and] call for minimal special material or equipment."[2] Here are some examples that show the range of job options that can be done from home:

- artist/craft making
- attorney
- bookkeeping/ accounting
- customer service
- data entry
- daycare facility/ babysitter
- DJ services
- financial advising
- hair styling
- handyman
- home inspection
- house cleaning/office cleaning
- insurance brokerage services
- IT consulting
- massage therapy
- medical case management
- online auction selling (such as eBay)
- pet care/dog walker
- photography/ videography
- private detective services
- proofreading
- property management
- real estate
- researching
- sales
- social media work
- survey/focus group participation
- tax preparation
- tech support
- telemarketing
- transcription
- tutoring
- verification by phone
- virtual assistant

> ## STOP! You Can't Do That from Home
>
> There are legal restrictions on certain types of home businesses. Before you set up any home-based venture, check your local and state laws and familiarize yourself with the laws and licensing requirements of your chosen profession. If you want to open your own home-based daycare center, you must understand your legal obligations for staffing, safety, and other matters. If you set out to sell your famous cupcakes to area restaurants, you must follow local and industry standards for food preparation—which will probably involve renting time in a commercial kitchen.

Narrow Your Options

With so many choices, how can you decide which work-from-home jobs are best for you? Start by considering work you're doing now or have done successfully in the past. What are your skills and abilities? Check the latest version of your résumé—and if you don't have a résumé, now is the time to draft one. Do you have desirable work experience that will translate to a new job working from home? The easiest solution is to find a home-based job similar or identical to your current or planned-for career. On the other hand, if you are looking for more variety, you can consider how your skills and interests might translate to a different type of work.

Either way, there are some excellent resources that can guide you to the types of jobs you should seek out. You can find them at your local public library or online. These publications outline some important details about occupations, including the levels of training and education required.

The *Occupational Outlook Handbook* (OOH), published by the U.S. Bureau of Labor Statistics, should be available at your library in print and can be found online at www.bls.gov/oco. Revised and updated every two years, the OOH includes detailed career information for all types of occupations, including a description of what workers do on the job, training and education needed, expected job prospects, salaries or wages, and working conditions. You'll also find links to information on state-by-state job markets, job search tips, and more.

O*NET, the Occupational Information Network, is sponsored by the U.S. Department of Labor and the Employment and Training Administration. The Network's public database, O*NET Online (www.onetonline.org) is a user-friendly resource with information on nearly one thousand occupations. Browse by occupation, by industry, by level of education needed, or by skill set. There is a lot of information and a lot of ways to search for it—so dedicate some time to browsing this reference.

Expand Your Skills

When you are trimming the list of possible work-at-home jobs, don't trim too far. In some cases, getting a certification or gaining some experience before you land a job can pay off. Maybe you need to learn new skills or specific business expertise; maybe you will have to pass an industry-specific exam. If so, see if your public library can help. Many libraries own software that teaches or tests specific skills—from an extensive program on studying for the GED, to a civil service job exam, to a practice exam for master carpentry.

Other Factors to Consider

Before you jump into the job ads, take a few minutes to assess your situation. Knowing your limitations will help you narrow your search.

Time

How much time can you devote to a work-from-home job? Do you have another job, classes, young children, or other time commitments? Be realistic about how many hours you would be able to work each day or week, and don't apply for or accept a job that requires more than you can give.

Availability

Are there other factors that might limit your work time? For example, if you need a computer to do your work, is that computer available to you any time, or do you have to share it with others in your home? If you are keeping an eye on your kids after school, how much work can you realistically do during those hours?

Workspace/Tools

Is there an appropriate place in your home for what you'd like to do—whether a home office with high-speed Internet or an area to set up a beauty salon station? Do you have everything you need to do the job, or can you get it? Do you need a dedicated telephone line, storage space for merchandise you are selling, or a vehicle to get you to clients' homes?

If your assessment reveals that your time, availability, or access to a workspace and tools may seriously limit your ability to make money working at home, then consider work-arounds—such as the alternative workplaces listed in chapter 2—or rethink your goal. Flexibility is crucial to working from home, even before you land a job.

Money: How Much Can You Make? ·····························

Undoubtedly, you picked up this book because of the title. You want to earn a living, or make some extra cash. But how much can you make when you work from home? The answer is as varied as the types of jobs you can find or create, but the following table shows what professionals earn in some positions that are frequently home-based.

Position	Median Hourly Wage	Median Annual Income
Computer support specialists (tech support)	$22.24	$46,260
Customer service representatives	$14.64	$30,460
Massage therapists	$16.78	$34,900
Medical transcriptionists	$15.82	$32,900
Pet care workers (trainers, groomers, dog walkers, etc.)	$ 9.40	$19,550

Source: Bureau of Labor Statistics Occupational Employment Statistics. Wages are for 2010 and are based on full-time employment.

Although these figures are not specifically for home-based positions, they should apply to all workers in these positions, both on-site and remote. There is a chance that a home-based employee may even earn a little more: a 2007 study found that a remote employee often makes a higher wage than one working the same job on-site.[3]

Keep in mind, though, that much of any salary is deducted for Medicare and Social Security, and for income taxes, before you receive it. When you see a job listed with an hourly wage or annual salary, you can use an online calculator to verify how much pay you'll be taking home (or, in this case, keeping at home with you while you work). The Hourly Wage Calculator at http://us.thesalarycalculator.co.uk/hourly.php is a good example. Type in the annual salary offered, and the calculator tells you what your daily, weekly, monthly, and annual take-home pay will be.

For those who plan to start their own home-based business, there is no sure way to estimate how much you will earn. You can, however, add up your costs of doing business in order to calculate how much you'll need to earn to turn a profit. And of course you won't be exempt from paying income taxes on your profit. Chapter 6 goes into more detail on this.

"There are financial advantages to working from home because I do not have transportation costs, costs for clothes, and costs for lunch. On the other hand, I keep my home cooler in the summer and warmer in the winter when I am home than when I am away, so electric and gas bills are higher than they would be if I were working at the office."

—*Diana Wellington, marketing manager*

Money Saved Is Money Earned

It's not just how much money you can make working from home—it's also how much you save by not working a traditional job. Telework Research Network has estimated that employees who work from home for just half of every workweek save an average $362 per year on gasoline alone.[4] Other possible savings include, on average, $7.37 a day on meals and $2.41 a day on work clothes. That adds up to $6,800 for these workers who spend just half of every week working from home.

How much do you think you could save by skipping your commute, simplifying your wardrobe, and avoiding cafeterias and vending machines? Fill out the Potential Savings chart below by assessing the costs of the last job you held (or applied for).

Potential Savings by Staying Home

Expense	Estimated Cost per Month
Commute (cost of wear and tear on car, gas, tolls, parking, public transportation)	
Clothing (cost of business attire, uniforms, dry cleaning)	
All lunches, snacks, coffee purchased	
Costs of being away from home (dog walker, afterschool childcare)	
Total	

After reading this chapter and considering your skills, abilities, and limitations for a work-from-home job, you should have a solid idea of the types of work you might look for, along with some preliminary knowledge of how to judge salary rates (and savings). In the next chapter, you can get an idea of what it's *really* like to work from home and learn some tips for making it work for you.

Notes

1. Rex Huppke, "Down with Pants, Up with Telecommuting," Chicagotribune.com, November 6, 2011.

2. Matthew Mariani, "Telecommuters," *Occupational Outlook Quarterly,* Fall 2000.

3. Bonnie Sue Gariety and Sherrill Shaffer, "Wage Differentials Associated with Working at Home," *Monthly Labor Review,* March 2007.

4. Margaret Price, "Work at Home: Take Pay Cut. Come Out Ahead," July 25, 2011. www.csmonitor.com/business/2011/0725/work-at-home-take-pay-cut.-come-out-ahead.

TWO

Tips and Tricks for Working from Home

To most of us who spend our days working on-site for employers, working from home sounds ideal—no commute, no cubicles, none of the stresses of an unpleasant workplace. But there's more to it than that, and you should have a realistic and complete idea of the changes that come with working from home before you start transforming your spare room into an office.

The Pros and Cons

There are definite advantages to working from home. Many of the negative aspects of everyday work don't exist, starting with your commute. And it is true that you'll be more independent, at least in some respects; a boss can't micromanage someone who is working remotely. Plus, chances are that you won't have to dress up. If you are working at home, you can stay in your fuzzy slippers all day if you like. But there are other benefits you may not have considered:

> *Employment opportunities.* Working from home greatly widens your opportunities for jobs. You can work for an employer in another state or even another country, because location isn't important.
>
> *Flexibility.* The lack of commuting time and sometimes flexible hours of working from home make it more likely that you can easily schedule two part-time home-based jobs, or a full-time job and a side business.
>
> *Productivity.* Management experts believe that employees who work from home get more done than those in a traditional job site—either because they put in more hours or because they don't have many of the distractions found in a typical workplace.
>
> *Cost savings.* As mentioned in chapter 1, you are likely to save money by working from home, and you may earn more as well.

It's Not for Everyone

According to the Telework Research Network, not every employee thinks working from home would suit him or her. In a 2009 survey of workers, 21 percent of those asked about their interest in working from home said they were not at all interested.

Source: www.teleworkresearchnetwork.com/ telecommuting-statistics/

These pros of staying home to work probably come as no surprise. But what about the downsides? There are some cons, and depending on your personality and work style, these may be deal breakers:

Isolation. Some people find that they thrive on daily interaction with others, so working alone doesn't suit them. If you get lonely when you are by yourself for eight hours or more at a stretch, or know that you work better and smarter when you can brainstorm in person with colleagues, be aware that the at-home, work-alone lifestyle may not be as fulfilling for you as a traditional job.

Learning curve. Whether you are starting a new job or moving a current position from office to home, how will you perform when learning a new task or skill? Without a supervisor or colleague present to literally show the way, you must be able to grasp and apply new information on your own (or over the phone). If this suits your learning style, go for it. If not, you will need to find a work-around.

Work/life balance. It can be difficult to draw a clear line between work and home when both are in the same place. You may find yourself checking messages after regular business hours, putting in some extra hours on the weekend, or even heading back to your desk after your family heads for bed. To maintain your sanity, your personal life, and your family's happiness, you must train yourself to close the office door at the end of every "shift"—even if that door doesn't actually exist.

Costs. Depending on the home-based job you have, you may be responsible for purchasing and providing your own resources. This might include the monthly cost of high-speed Internet, shipping costs, office supplies and equipment, and even travel. This obviously applies to any start-up business, but if you are looking for employment, make sure you have a clear understanding

of your responsibilities before you accept a job—
especially if the position is part-time or low paying.

Resources. As with costs of your office, you may not have
access to resources such as tech support or ordering
supplies. These functions, normally handled by your
employer, may require extra time and effort, which are
not "on the clock."

Limitations. Not all work-from-home jobs offer flexibility.
Some are not very different from traditional jobs, with
employees expected to work set hours, attend regular
meetings (remotely), and so on.

Are You a Work-from-Home Type?

According to Adecco, a large staffing company, good telecommuters thrive on their driven natures and personal freedom and
are able to create a work/life balance without strict guidelines; are
self-starters and high achievers who produce strong results with a
minimum of supervision; are technologically self-sufficient; and
have the personal networks, knowledge, and experience to deal on
their own with problems that arise.[1]

> "I miss having physical coworker interaction, both work and
> personal (like birthday celebrations). Another negative is that I
> sometimes work longer hours than I otherwise might because I
> have no set starting or quitting time."
>
> —*Karen Karcher, IT application administrator*

How many of the characteristics in the Work Personality Assessment chart do you have? The more times you select "That's me!"
the more likely you are to succeed in a home-based job.

Work Personality Assessment

Personality Trait	That's Me!	Not So Much . . .
Disciplined		
Self-starter		
Independent worker		
Good on the telephone		
Organized		
Honest		

Your Workspace

Consider where you can work within your home. Do you need room for merchandise or supplies or just a standard home office with computer, printer, and some file cabinets? How important is it for what you'll be doing—and the type of worker you are—to be able to work quietly and without interruption? Not everyone has the luxury of transforming a garage into a studio, or even of choosing among available rooms for a home office. Regardless of the size and layout of your home, try to consider options beyond the obvious.

For example, consider Emily, a freelance writer who lived alone and bought a two-bedroom condominium. Rather than turn the small second bedroom into her office, as you might expect, she opted to transform approximately a third of her living room into her office. She knew she would be spending a lot of time at her desk, and she wanted to enjoy the large windows and airy space of the main room. She arranged the furniture in the room to distinguish the office and the leisure area clearly, and when she wanted to remove herself from the temptation to work long hours there was always the "den"—that smaller second bedroom.

Alternatively, you can transform a walk-in closet, a sun porch, or an attic into a home office. If you have a nook like this, test it out first to make sure it is comfortable enough, pleasant enough, and large enough to suit your purposes. Like Emily, you may be spending a lot of time there.

There are numerous other matters to take into account when scoping out a home workspace:

Are there enough electrical outlets to support all of your office equipment?

If you will be using a landline telephone or fax machine (some industries still do), is there a phone jack nearby?

If you will be using your mobile phone, do you get clear reception in that area of your home? Test it several times to make sure.

How quiet is the area? Will you be able to conduct business calls without distracting noises from household members, pets, or outdoor nuisances like traffic?

Is the area comfortable in terms of square footage, temperature and ventilation, and lighting?

Do you have adequate storage space? Keep in mind that the things you don't need everyday access to, including older files or extra office supplies, can be stowed in other parts of your home if necessary.

Is there a way to "shut the office door" to help you maintain a work/life balance and keep confidential information secure?

"I started out working at my dining room table because the light is really good there. But very soon the table was filled up with beads and other working materials, and I realized that wasn't going to work. So I do all the work at a desk in my home office. I added a light and have storage for all the little components I work with."

—*Roslyn Broder, owner of RedAvaDesigns jewelry business*

Furnish with Frugality

Once you've settled on the area of your home to work in, you can determine what you need to fill it up. Assuming you need a home office, the furnishings should be obvious. Any necessary furniture you don't already have you should try to get as cheaply as possible—at least until you're certain that working from home is going to suit you. You can browse Craigslist or garage sales for temporary furniture and storage options, or ask around to see if someone you know has items you can borrow or take. But don't just "make do" with a physically uncomfortable setup, or you could pay the price in back pain, eyestrain, or worse.

It seems that most desks sold today—at least those designed with home offices in mind—provide only a desktop, with minimal drawers or storage options. You'll probably need to add a filing cabinet, and perhaps shelving, a bulletin board, upright file holders, or whatever system works best for you to keep the things you need most at your fingertips.

Alternatives to "Home" When Working from Home

Maybe you want to work from home but your situation won't allow it. If you want to earn money without commuting to a job every day, but your own home is too small, noisy, crowded, lonely, or otherwise not conducive to getting work done, consider these alternatives:

Public library. It's free, Internet access and probably Wi-Fi are available, there may be rooms where you can meet with others, and you can spend as much time as you want there, digging into the numerous resources. The public library is not, however, a place to make phone calls.

College library. Just like the public library.

Coffee shop/bookstore. This usually means the cost of a small purchase. Wi-Fi is becoming more common at these locations. You can meet with others, though not in private rooms. You can make a few phone calls, but you'll have to keep your voice down.

Shared office/rented desk. You pay rent monthly, you can expect all the communication tools you will need (Internet, phone, etc.), and conference rooms may be available. Basically, you get all the benefits of working in an employer's office—but each may come with a price tag.

Avoid the Three Danger Zones

When you are working from home, without the constant support of coworkers and a manager down the hall, you may find yourself slipping in job performance and even quality of life. The key is to look beyond your solo desk and (1) keep yourself motivated and on track to ensure your work gets done, (2) remain professional even without those daily supports, and (3) keep yourself connected to the outside world.

Stay Motivated

Everyone who considers working from home has their own reasons—but those reasons rarely include the work itself. Once you find yourself enjoying the freedom and flexibility of conducting business while keeping one eye on your kids, the television, or the oven timer, don't forget to do your job.

The key to success is to set daily goals, stick to a schedule, and give yourself rewards to stay motivated. You can use any system that works for you, as long as you set and meet realistic "to-dos." This ensures that you get your job done and make your employer (if you have one) happy. With any new job, it may take a while to understand your responsibilities. But with effort, attention, and action (make it your priority to find answers fast), you'll figure them out. At that point, use this method to stay on track and stay motivated at the same time:

Keep an ongoing list of your tasks and responsibilities. If you have the same task every day, such as answering customer service calls, continue to list it.

Break down any complex tasks or projects into smaller "chunks." Schedule the time and date when each task or stage of a project must be completed.

Reward yourself for completed tasks. This is where your motivation comes in. Choose a reward that appeals to you, such as a ten-minute snack break for every two hours worked, a walk around the neighborhood, a game of Angry Birds, or something bigger for a longer-term accomplishment. Some people might be motivated by calculating how much income they are earning this pay period.

Your daily to-do list and schedule should keep you on track. Some workers do best when they stick to the same daily schedule, working the same hours every day and maybe starting each day answering e-mail before moving on to the first task. Others who prefer to work at home are eager to get away from this "rut" and do better if every day is different. If the job allows, they can work different hours each day and tackle projects as they choose. In either case, check that ongoing list of your to-dos and avoid procrastinating—you are ultimately responsible for meeting your employer's (or your own business's) needs and expectations.

Your employer may provide or require specific software for scheduling or tracking projects, such as Microsoft Outlook, so that colleagues or managers can access your projects. But for maintaining your own to-do list and schedule, consider which of these types best fits your preferences and work style:

> *Computer- or Internet-based solutions.* Your computer comes with a calendar program, which likely includes a tasks or to-do component. If any part of this program doesn't suit you, there are many others available online or as free downloads. E-mail programs such as Gmail include calendars and task lists as well, and free Internet-based services allow you to access your calendar and lists from any location.
>
> *Smartphone app.* Any smartphone comes with a basic calendar application installed that offers reminders and

alerts. You can use this to set up to-dos for each day or search available apps for more robust programs.

Paper calendar. If you prefer paper to electronic documents, you still have plenty of options. You can create a system that works for you, such as a large desk calendar with room to write in tasks for each day. You might invest in a more robust system such as a Franklin Covey planner.

Paper lists. To keep a simple but updateable to-do list in writing, you can design a system that uses a multipage notebook, download free task-list forms, or create your own.

White board or chalkboard. This is ideal for those who want their schedule right in front of them at all times. It's easy to keep updated and hard to ignore.

The bottom line is, you won't be employed for long if you don't complete your assigned work. That's your real motivation.

Stay Professional

After days and weeks spent working alone, without colleagues surrounding your cubicle, frequent team meetings, and unexpected visits from your boss, you may find your professionalism slipping. This can be a problem as you relax into a home routine where lines are blurred between when you are an employee or proprietor of your own business and when you are a spouse, dog's best friend, or pajama-clad television enthusiast. Here are some tips for staying businesslike when you're conducting business:

Keep regular business hours. If your job requires you to work during specific hours, be available and prepared

during that time. When your phone rings or an e-mail or
instant message pops up, you should be not only alert
but prepared to look up information or answer whatever
question comes your way. When your manager or client
expects you to be available for a quick conference call,
it's best to be in front of a computer with clear telephone
reception—not at the grocery store.

Keep it quiet. When you are working in a home that includes
other family members, pets, or even distracting outside
noises, figure out a way to block sounds when you're
on the phone or in meetings. Your dedicated workspace
should be remote enough that you can enjoy some peace
and quiet—so that you can concentrate on your work
and sound professional over the phone.

Be organized. With a new workspace, you need to figure out
how to sort, stow, and store important documents and
items. Keep your work materials and supplies contained
to your desk or work area (even after you decide to carry
your laptop into the backyard for a working lunch), and
leave current project files where you can access them
quickly and easily. This helps you appear professional
even if no one ever sees your workspace—with the
added bonus of keeping you efficient. A disorganized
workspace costs you time and effort in tracking down
documents or other materials.

Interrupt interruptions. When you start working from home,
it can be difficult to convince some family members and
friends that you are really working. These well-meaning
folks may need to be taught that just because you're
at home doesn't mean you're available for a nice long
chat, an invitation to a leisurely lunch, or even helping

out with their daytime errands. Be firm in turning down requests and offers, and keep phone conversations short. They'll get the message soon enough.

Give voice to professionalism. Sound professional when you answer the phone during your work hours. If you don't have a dedicated mobile phone or landline for your work and are not sure about an incoming call, play it safe and answer as if it is a work call. Also, make sure you record a voicemail greeting that identifies you by name, title, and company.

Look the Part

If you need help sounding and acting professional when working from home, one standard piece of advice is to dress in business attire to stay in the right frame of mind. Another, perhaps easier, tip is to hang a mirror in your work area and look at yourself while you're on the telephone.

Stay Connected

When you are working from home, you lose a vital daily connection to colleagues and, in some cases, to the outside world. It is important to make an effort to stay connected to those you work with in order to know what's happening in your department, organization, and industry—and simply to stay sharp when you don't have a water cooler to hang around. Here are some tips for staying connected:

Be proactive. Don't rely on other people (including your manager) to keep you informed. Busy professionals today are more likely to forget to share information, especially if your organization doesn't have much experience using employees who work remotely. So make it a priority to touch base with your manager, colleagues, and anyone else who might be "in the know," and proactively ask what's happening and what you might need to be informed about. Check meeting schedules, even if you have to ask, to make sure you are participating in appropriate conversations.

Use communications technology. As a home-based worker, your telephone and your Internet connections are your lifeline to the world of work. Use all the tools your company offers, including instant messaging, Skype, and video- or web-conferencing tools.

> "I keep in touch with coworkers via instant messages, e-mail, and phone. We have online meetings via WebEx. And I get more done because nobody is dropping by my 'cube' to see how I'm doing."
>
> —*Heather Z. Hutchins, writer*

Meet up. Even if you never visit your employer's or a client's office, you can find ways to stay in touch with the business world. Join a professional association (ask if your employer will cover the membership fee) and attend local meetings. You can also browse Meetup.com to find some professional groups in your area. You'll be surprised how specific these groups can get.

Stay social. If you find yourself too isolated by working from home, broaden your after-hours social life. Start scheduling more activities in your nonwork hours, whether with friends, family, neighbors, or strangers.

Sign up for a class, join a running or walking club, or start a book group. Try to get out of the house and socialize several times a week, and write activities on your calendar to help ensure that you go.

Now that you have some idea of the challenges you'll face when you start working from your home, it's time to start actively looking for a way to reach your goal and give you a chance to find out for yourself what it's like to succeed when working from home.

Note

1. From "How to Use Telecommuting to Cut Costs," Adecco, www.adeccousa.com/knowledgecenter/employer-articles/Pages/Thinkingoutsidetheoffice.aspx.

Part II

Working for an Employer from Home

THREE

How to Look for Telecommuting Jobs

Good jobs are tough to find, and a good work-from-home job is even tougher. Despite the fact that more organizations are offering more employees the option of working remotely, your job search is likely to take a while and to involve many ads answered, applications completed, and résumés submitted. Nevertheless, the jobs are out there—so don't get discouraged.

There are so many types of work that can be done from home (or outside of a company office or workplace). But how should you go about finding the right opportunity for you? The short answer is, just as you would begin your search for a first-time job, but with some subtle differences.

> "My company kept moving farther and farther away from my home—the office is currently 75 miles away. I was very fortunate that my boss allowed me to telecommute. Plus, my job works from basically anywhere with an Internet connection."
>
> —*Karen Karcher, IT application administrator*

Step 1: Do Your Research

Ideally, your job search will start with some online research to see what types of work-from-home jobs are available, the qualifications employers are looking for, the hours and pay, and any other details you can gather. Doing this first allows you to target your search on the basis of job market—from crafting your résumé to address actual positions, to picking up words and phrases to use in interviews, and even to negotiating your salary before accepting a job.

General and Specific Job Boards

You'll find home-based jobs sprinkled throughout standard online job boards, from the general giants such as Careerbuilder.com and Monster.com to industry-specific sites like Accounting.com or Dice.com (for technology professionals). Take time to search out the best online job boards for you, and read through the ads to note the following about the types of positions you're interested in:

Most common job titles. Note which you'd like to include in a search of online postings, mention while networking, and list as goals.

Keywords and phrases to use. These are important for searching online postings and writing your résumé and cover letter—and even for use during interviews.

Salary and benefits. Track these for use when you negotiate your pay.

Average hours per week and other requirements. Get a feel for the state of the work-from-home jobs. Are they mostly part-time? Can you set your own hours?

Skills/experience required. An overview of requirements gives you an idea of how qualified you are.

On any job board with search capabilities, filter the jobs by choosing your search words and phrases wisely. Use a job title or key phrase, along with a term such as *remote, virtual, off-site, telecommute,* or *telework.* And be sure to visit websites that specialize in listing home-based jobs. Here are some that do:

Worldwide Work at Home. This site uses Indeed.com
   job listings. It is searchable by a limited number of
   professions, including data entry, transcription, and web
   design and development, but it also provides a list of the
   most recent leads. www.worldwideworkathome.com/
   jobboard.html

Work at Home Jobs. Jobs here are unique to this site and are
   posted by organizations and individuals, complete with
   pay ranges. Some are projects, and some are permanent
   positions. Browse by keyword and desired pay. www
   .workathomejobs.org

Working Home Guide. Employers pay to post work-from-
   home positions on this job board, which lists full-time,
   part-time, contract, and temporary jobs in a wide variety
   of fields. http://jobs.workinghomeguide.com/a/jbb/find
   -jobs/

WAHM.com. WAHM (an acronym for work-at-home moms)
   is an online magazine that uses Indeed.com job listings.
   Use keywords *work at home* and type in your location.
   www.wahm.com/jobs.html

Work at Home Careers. The site's owner claims to prescreen
   the job postings on this site, which can be browsed
   by profession (sales, telephone reps, etc.). www.work
   athomecareers.com/workathomejobs/

Flex Jobs. Job seekers pay a monthly fee to access this site's
   prescreened listings of work-from-home openings. The

more than seven thousand legitimate jobs on the site include unique posts and those culled from other online sources, all offering at least some flexibility, including freelance. Fee options (2012) include $14.95 per month and $49.95 per year. www.flexjobs.com

Once you've studied (and taken notes on) postings for work-from-home jobs, you'll have the tools you need to conduct your search.

Be Smart about Scams

If you are even a little bit savvy, you'll see in your research that there are plenty of scams and rip-offs sprinkled through work-from-home job listings. Because so many people are interested in working from home—and in earning big bucks—con artists are constantly coming up with ways to prey on them. Any ad that promises an unbelievable amount of money per day or per week is questionable. Any job opening that requires you to pay in advance for information, customer lists, materials, or simply for applying should definitely be avoided. The table below offers some basic tips for identifying scams.

Once your résumé is posted with online job boards, you may receive offers for at-home work via e-mail. These too can be scams (and likely are), so use common sense when evaluating how legitimate they may be.

If you are not sure a posting is legitimate, do some online research. Check the company website to see if it is an established business, and then look up the organization with the Better Business Bureau at www.bbb.org/us/find-business-reviews. Finally, browse the Internet for any complaints or legal actions, using a general search engine such as Google or review sites such as Yelp.com.

How to Spot a Scam

Signs of a Legitimate Job Posting	Signs of a Scam
Real job title or position names, such as "data entry professional"	No job title. Vague reference to working from home for extra money
Pay mentioned matches your research finding	Pay mentioned seems too good to be true
Steps for responding include sending résumé or filling out application	Steps for responding include sending personal information such as Social Security number or bank account numbers
E-mail address for inquiries matches company name (info@ xyzcorp.com)	E-mail address for inquiries is generic, such as yahoo.com
Posting includes basic requirements for experience and skills	Posting assures you that no experience is necessary
If company name is provided, you can find a website for the organization	No company name or industry mentioned

Step 2: Work Your Networks

Any effective job search should include some serious networking—both online and in person. Organizations don't always advertise open positions, whether they are work-from-home or not, and networking can be a way to discover these "hidden" job opportunities. It can also get you a foot in the door if you discover an acquaintance who can introduce or recommend you.

The fact is, when you enlist the help of friends, colleagues, and even people you just met, you increase the power of your job search tremendously. According to sociologist Mark Granovetter, the people who can be the most helpful are those we don't know well. Granovetter told *Forbes* magazine that "informal contacts" account for almost 75 percent of all successful job searches. In other words, if your best friend doesn't know of a job for you, it's more likely that his neighbor—or his neighbor's boss—might help.

So make connections with people you know and the people *they* know, and with people in the industry and the organizations you want to work in—and it's likely you'll connect to some major help in your job search.

Employed? Take It Home

If you are currently working a job that you think you can do from home, try to convince your employer to give it a try. Outline your "sales pitch" in advance, stressing the benefits to the organization of telecommuting (e.g., frees up your workspace and equipment) and your strengths as an employee—especially those personality traits included in the Work Personality Assessment in chapter 2. Propose a three- or six-month trial period, or, if your boss or human resources manager is hesitant, suggest a period in which you split your time between home and office.

Need stronger arguments? Send your human resources manager to the Telework Research Network website for a list of benefits to your company, including a ready-made implementation plan and telecommuting policy: www.telework researchnetwork.com/purpose.

You won't earn extra money by transforming your current job to a work-from-home position, but you may save hundreds of dollars each month (see chapter 1).

Online Networking

Face-to-face networking is crucial, but you can also turbo-boost the number of professionals you meet and connect with by using social media websites, online discussion groups, and other web-based tools. LinkedIn is the undisputed champion of online networking for professionals. Facebook, a more personal site, can often be used to your advantage, as can a Twitter account. Also try Meetup.com. Online discussion forums on sites for appropriate professional associations, including "affinity groups" such as the American Assembly for Men in Nursing or the California Association of Black Lawyers, are valuable for specialized interests. And don't forget the website for your alumni association.

Most, if not all, of these sites require you to sign up with some personal information and create a user name and password for future use. Remember to keep track of these names and passwords so that you can get back into a site once you register.

The Power of LinkedIn

LinkedIn should be among the top bookmarked sites for any job seeker. It is designed specifically so that business professionals can network, and it provides a wealth of information (sometimes available only for actual wealth) for those researching hiring managers and organizations.

With LinkedIn, you create a personal profile, then link to other people on the site to create your own network. You can only view complete profiles of (or send a message, or "InMail," to) those you are personally connected to—unless you pay LinkedIn a monthly fee. However, you can always see basic identifying information for anyone on the site.

If you are not "linked" already, it's easy to get started:

1. Visit www.linkedin.com.
2. Take plenty of time to craft your profile carefully. This will serve as your online résumé, an introduction, and an identifier.

3. Use as many keywords as you can in your profile—it is searchable by other LinkedIn users, and recruiters have been known to browse the site to find ideal job candidates.

4. Invite everyone you know to join your network: former and current work colleagues and managers, friends, classmates, family, neighbors. But focus on those who might be in a position to help you search: well-connected people or anyone who has anything to do with your industry.

5. To find contacts you know, search through provided lists of company employees and university graduates. Also try browsing the connections of those you connect to, to see if you can find mutual acquaintances. Note that, ethically, you can connect only to people you already know, even if you only met that person once.

6. When you invite someone to join your LinkedIn network, always include a personal note, no matter how brief.

7. Once your profile is complete and you have established some connections, seek recommendations from those you have worked for. Consider which of your acquaintances are most beneficial to your job hunt, then send each a brief but polite message through LinkedIn requesting a personal recommendation about specific skills, knowledge, or strengths. All recommendations will show up on your profile for visitors to see. An added benefit: if your former manager writes you a recommendation, all of *his* connections will be notified, drawing their attention to you.

8. Update your profile regularly, or post your latest accomplishment, activity, or insight. Those you are

> connected to will be notified of your new status,
> keeping you on their radar.

As you build your LinkedIn connections, you will be able to see second- and third-level connections—the people that your connections are connected to, and the people whom *those* connections are connected to. You can see at a glance the strength of weak ties, when you see that your former work colleague is connected to a hiring manager at the company you want to work for. You can ask your common connection for an introduction to that inside connection, or you can "upgrade" your LinkedIn account, paying a monthly fee for the ability to send a specific number of InMails to secondary connections.

LinkedIn does include a job search area, but the true value of this site for a job seeker lies in the wealth of organizational and employee information available and the possibility of reaching out to connections of connections. In fact, if you have first-, second-, or third-tier connections to a company, it will show up in the job posting.

Networking in Person

Before you attend any formal networking events, work your personal network. Contact people in your life to let them know you're looking for a job working from home, what type of job you want, and how they might help you. Get in touch with extended family members, friends, neighbors, current and former work colleagues, former classmates, fellow members of your church, clubs, and civic organizations, and everyone else you know. Ask these people to spread the word of your job search to *their* networks. You might feel uncomfortable approaching people you haven't spoken to in a long time, or those you don't know very well. But once you get over your initial apprehension, you'll find that businesspeople find networking a perfectly natural activity.

Next, consider what types of people may best help you find a home-based job in your field, and where you might find them. For example, if you are pursuing a job as a tech support professional, what groups or associations might you join? What meetings might website designers attend? When is the next national conference related to your industry coming to town? Do your research before you choose a local networking venue.

Prepare Your Elevator Pitch

When you are networking for a job, it is best to have an elevator pitch planned and rehearsed. An elevator pitch is a brief—no more than two-minute—explanation that you can state in the time it takes to share an elevator ride. Practice a pitch that tells who you are and what you want, so you can be ready to introduce yourself clearly and succinctly. Include the fact that you specifically want a position that allows you to work from home.

Online Resources for Locating In-Person Networking

Here's an easy way to find local groups of like-minded professionals who meet in person: browse the Internet.

For example, at Meetup.com you can enter your town and area of interest to find groups that meet regularly in-person. Whether your interest is marketing or skiing, the groups you find exist solely to help you meet and network with like-minded people in your area.

LinkedIn also offers a multitude of groups, only some of which meet in person. Click on "Groups" at the top of any LinkedIn page, then "Groups Directory." When you search the groups, select "Networking Groups" and type in the category and keywords that fit your job search.

You can also browse thousands of professional associations by profession and industry in Weddle's Association Directory at www .weddles.com/associations/index.cfm.

Network through Volunteering

Volunteer work offers an ideal opportunity to expand your network while learning or demonstrating the skills you'll use in your home-based job. Looking for a marketing position? Offer to write news releases, promote fundraising events, or create a marketing plan for a local charity. Aiming for a home-based sales position? Sign up to help with fundraising efforts.

Not sure of your career path? Volunteer for a community or national charity, and meet professionals from all walks of life. Find out what they do for a living, what it's like, and whether it would be a good fit for you—and add the volunteer experience to your résumé.

You can also add new skills or strengthen others through the right volunteer position. Want to polish your telephone skills? Volunteer to contact members for the next renewal drive. Interested in using your second language for a translating career? Many charities need on-site translators for verbal or written work. Want to gain some leadership experience? Sign up to lead a committee or serve on the board.

Steps for In-Person Networking Events

Not everyone is a natural networker. Fortunately, there are strategies you can use to make the most of "face time."

Before You Go

> *Craft—and practice—your elevator pitch.* This may be different for different networking opportunities.

Have a couple of conversation points ready—perhaps on the latest news within the industry. When in doubt, ask the other person about herself.

Set one specific goal before each event. Examples: Are you looking for a job lead? Someone to review your résumé and job search plan? Tips on breaking into the industry?

While You're There

Work the room. No matter how shy or uncomfortable you feel, approach people and introduce yourself.

Find the "movers and shakers." Use your powers of observation and the goodwill of the meeting's organizer or greeter to ask questions and find the people at the event who are most likely to help you—whether you think they are the officers of the association, employees of certain companies you are prospecting, or "big names" in the industry.

Be efficient with your time and with others' time. This includes being prepared to disengage yourself politely from unproductive conversations.

Don't ask anyone to hire you. Instead, ask for their help and advice with your search.

Ask for business cards. If you discuss anything you'd like to follow up on, jot down a note to yourself on their card.

When You Get Home

Review your experience. Look through the business cards you collected, and add any notes you may have missed while the event is still fresh in your mind. Invite the most promising contacts you made to join your LinkedIn network.

Organize your contacts. Ideally, you should do this
electronically so that your growing database of job-
search contacts is searchable. You can use Microsoft
Outlook or create an Excel spreadsheet (see the Sample
Networking Contact Tracking System below). Include
the person's contact information, title, and company,
where and when you met him (every time if ongoing),
and any notes about his background or expertise that
might aid your search.

Follow up. Initiate a second contact if you said you would—
or even if you didn't, in the case of the most valuable
contacts you made.

- If you agreed to follow up with someone you met,
  call or e-mail the person within a day or two, while
  your encounter is still fresh in her mind.

- Suggest a prescheduled phone call or an in-person
  meeting as an opportunity to discuss your goals. If
  she is amenable to a one-on-one meeting, suggest
  having coffee near her office or home, and pick up
  the tab.

- Again, don't ask for a job—ask for advice, industry
  information, leads, and other relevant information.

- Be sure to open that follow-up conversation with a
  big thank-you, and end it with an offer to help the
  person you are talking to. Networking is a two-way
  street.

Evaluate your experience. Review the networking that you
did and what you'd like to do differently the next time
you go out.

Sample Networking Contact Tracking System

Name	Company	Title	Where Met	Follow-up
Sandra Anders	ABC Corporation	Regional sales	5/12/12 library meeting	Send article on Google marketing
Sarah Jones	Meteor Marketing	Director of sales	5/12/12 library meeting	None
Fred Fredericks	Premium Coffee Co.	Sales manager	May meeting— NSWA	Call for information int.

Step 3: Hit the Job Fairs

Job fairs are hosted by colleges and universities, communities and profession-specific groups, and consortiums. Many job fairs are extremely general, with a wide range of employers and positions. Others are targeted to specific industries or professions, such as a communications technology job fair. When searching for a job that allows you to work from home, skip any fair hosted by a local politician, political candidate, or community organization; these are likely to offer only positions in the immediate area. A fair that casts a wider net is much more apt to include telecommuting jobs.

If you are plugged in to the job-seekers' network, you automatically learn about upcoming job fairs through online forums and groups; they are advertised on career sites, and fellow members of your job support group or networking circle will tell you. You may also find out through local newspapers, bulletin boards, and your local unemployment office.

Before You Show Up

It is important to do your homework before you attend a job fair. This includes more than simply preregistering and ironing your best shirt:

- ▸ Find out which prospective employers will be participating, and select those you want to be sure to meet. Take time to do some online research to check out each one before the fair.
- ▸ If a map of the fair is available, literally plot your route.
- ▸ Know what you want from this particular fair, and have an appropriate elevator speech prepared. Understand that your time with a prospective employer may be extremely limited, and come prepared to make that time count.
- ▸ Rehearse your elevator speech and practice answering interview questions.
- ▸ Select the business attire you plan to wear, clean and prepare it, and try it on to make sure everything is ready.
- ▸ Have a professional-looking briefcase ready to hold résumés and portfolio, and use it to carry the materials you gather at the fair.
- ▸ Have plenty of copies of appropriate résumés and business cards ready.
- ▸ If you have a portfolio, bring that as well.

Working the Fair

If possible, get to the job fair early. Depending on the fair, there may be long lines to get in as well as lines at each organization's table or booth. Arriving well before the start time ensures that you get through registration quickly and can start working your map route, visiting your list of "top picks" first. (Don't forget to check at registration to see if there are any last-minute additions of hiring companies.) At each table or booth you visit, try these strategies:

 ▸ Pick up the take-away handouts they provide, and review if possible before engaging in conversation.
 ▸ When you're ready to talk—or when the recruiter makes eye contact—greet her and give a firm handshake along with your elevator speech. Keep in mind that the employees working the job fair are probably not the hiring managers; they are human resource professionals who are screeners for the company.
 ▸ Take notes during each conversation or interview so you are able to keep them straight when you get home.
 ▸ Make sure you get a business card or contact information for everyone you might want to follow up with—and give them yours.
 ▸ Take advantage of the pool of job seekers, and network with them as well. Find out what's working best for them.

After the Fair

When you get home from the job fair, organize the business cards and information you collected. Input all relevant details into your contact tracking system. And be sure to write thank-you e-mails or notes to each recruiter you talked to—and send those thank-yous within a day or two.

Step 4: Zero In on a Target

Once you get a solid lead on a position or organization you'd like to work for, it's time to become a hardcore researcher—and unearth relevant facts that will help you narrow your search, find the right contacts, and build your application before you take part in your first interview. The more you know about the organization in advance, the better off you are.

More Research

If you didn't already do this sufficiently when you began the job hunt, researching employers by industry, corporate stability, and other factors can help you focus your search—and possibly pursue an opportunity that has not been advertised yet. There are three sets of tools you can use for this research:

Public Library Databases
Check with your local pubic library to see which databases it subscribes to that might contain company information. Most libraries have subscription databases in which you can find company information, often with live links so you can just click through to their website. Databases include *ReferenceUSA, Million Dollar Directory,* and *LexisNexis Library Express.*

Websites
Of course, the Internet provides plenty of information on companies by industry, location, and other factors. Try these sites to start:

Hoover's. Hoover's is the granddaddy of company information, now online with free, up-to-date, and detailed information on more than 50,000 companies. It includes privately owned companies, which is rare on other sites. You can access some information for free, but much of it is fee-based. www.hoovers.com

Jigsaw. Jigsaw is primarily a source for employee directories within companies, but you can browse the site by industry, company name, state, or city to find an extensive list of companies. www.jigsaw.com

Inc. Inc. Magazine provides basic information on what it found to be the "fastest growing" organizations within each industry. www.inc.com/inc5000/list/2012/

Guidestar. Guidestar includes a searchable directory of nonprofit organizations. www.guidestar.org

Fortune. Fortune magazine's list of best companies to work for is updated annually. http://money.cnn.com/magazines/fortune/bestcompanies/

List of Lists. The List of Lists (originally Price's List of Lists) is a database of ranked listings of companies, people, and resources maintained by Special Issues. www.specialissues.com/lol/

Personal contacts.

Work your network. As you attend meetings and events, or introduce (and reintroduce) yourself to others during your job search, ask about what companies you should include in your search. If you're talking to someone in your targeted industry, ask where they work, where they've worked in the past, and which are the "local leader" companies in that industry. And if you're talking to someone who is not in your targeted industry, it is still worth finding out if they have any contacts or knowledge about that field—you never know.

Focused Research on a Company

The second aspect of researching an organization comes when you have decided to contact a company about a job opening, or after you are invited to an interview. The timing for this type of research is crucial, because the more you know about the organization, the industry, and even the individuals you may interview with, the more likely you are to stand out from your competition and impress your interviewers. Research the following topics before you customize your résumé and cover letter, before you visit the company at a job fair, or before your initial interview.

History, Size, and Scope of the Organization

Search the "about us" section of the organization's own website. If the organization you are targeting is owned by a larger corporation, has changed its name, or has a second identity, try a Google search on additional names to see what information you might unearth. In addition to a broad overview of the company, you may be able to figure out values, corporate culture, and even key words to use in writing or conversation.

Products and Services

Studying the company's products and services is a great way to familiarize yourself with what exactly the company does and imagine how you might fit in. Memorize product names or at least categories before you interview.

Financial Health and Stability

This can be found on a variety of financial sites. If the organization is publicly traded (owned by stockholders), you can easily check its financial performance. Start with the EDGAR database of the U.S. Securities & Exchange Commission (www.sec.gov). And Yahoo!

Finance (http://finance.yahoo.com) compiles financial news on specific publicly traded companies; just type the company name into the search field. Also check the organization's own website for an annual report, which will include the year's financial performance. Nonprofit organizations as well as publicly traded ones may post their reports online.

Organizational Chart and Managerial Staff

Use the company's website and brochures to find out who the major players are as well as who you might be working with in the open position. Note names and titles before heading in for an interview.

What's New/Press Releases

Glean the latest news about the company from its website for excellent points to bring up in an interview or cover letter. Past news provides an instant time line for developments, product releases, even new hires—and demonstrates what the company thinks is newsworthy.

Other Recent Company News

Search on sites for industry trade journals, local newspapers, and perhaps professional associations. A carefully worded general search may yield recent news articles and announcements as well.

Industry News

It's a good idea to read up on general news about your profession, industry, and area throughout your job search. That way you'll be knowledgeable and insightful on cue when you unexpectedly meet a potential contact, while you're networking, and especially when you're applying for and interviewing for positions. Here are some simple tips for staying in the know:

▶ Select one to three sources of industry-specific news (most likely trade journals) and at least skim every issue or update. If a publication is not available online for free, see if you can sign up for a trial subscription, borrow hard copies from a subscriber you know, or consider sharing the cost of a subscription with one or more fellow job seekers.

▶ Bookmark the website of a trade association. Check for recent updates to discussion forums or press releases. If you are a member, you may be able to get automatic news e-mails.

▶ Join a profession- or industry-specific group on LinkedIn, and monitor the discussion forums.

▶ Scan the headlines in your local or national newspaper every day. (Do this online for free.) This will prepare you for "small talk" at networking events or targeted comments in an interview situation. Job hunters can sometimes be isolated—be able to demonstrate that you know what's happening in the world.

Researching Individuals

Once you have pinpointed a specific organization to pursue, remember to include the hiring managers and other potential interviewers in your research. This level of investigation helps you address (and customize) your cover letter and résumé to a specific hiring manager when answering a "blind" job ad. It can also make networking easier: if you want an informational interview from a specific company, you can find out the most appropriate person to talk to. Finally, when preparing for an interview you can find out more about the people you'll be speaking with.

The two main places to look up titles, names, and contact information for employees within a company are that company's website and LinkedIn. You might also try a Google search on the person's name (if you know it) and company to see if any news items come up.

Keep in mind, too, that if you are going in for an in-person interview (or even a telephone interview), it is likely that the interviewer has also checked *you* out on LinkedIn and through a general Google search.

Get Help from the Pros

There is no reason to conduct a job search on your own. There is an army of agencies and recruiters out there, making their living matching up people like you with employers who need you. Similarly, knowledgeable professionals at job centers and your public library can provide resources and recommendations that will help put your search on the fast track.

Temp Agencies

Like traditional jobs, work-from-home jobs can be found through employment agencies, including temporary agencies. Temp jobs are available in practically every industry and include those similar to permanent jobs that can be performed at home. When an agency hires you to work a temp or contract position, you report to the agency, not the organization you are doing work for. You fill out an application (and likely a mountain of other paperwork) with the agency, send your timesheets to them, and receive your paychecks from them. You can sign up with as many temp agencies as you like when you are job hunting; you will probably see many of them listed in job postings, or you can search the Internet for local temp agencies.

Recruiters

There are plenty of employment agencies that handle finding temp workers *and* permanent employees. If you are interested in either, signing up with these agencies for help finding at-home work will save you a little time. Recruiters, or headhunters, try to match your skills and experience with their clients' needs—so the client pays the fee and the recruiter does the hard work of finding you a job. This may sound ideal, but in reality many people who rely on recruiters don't see much action. Unless you have some much-sought-after skills, this process may move slowly or not at all.

Free Information

The art and science of looking for a job change constantly. You can find free resources and guidance in a couple of places. Many communities have a job center funded by local government, and all communities have a public library. Visit the library—and get a library card if you don't have one—to access free workshops and classes for job seekers, subscription databases that will turbo-boost your research capabilities, training and testing software, and more.

Now that you have some ideas for finding jobs that allow you to work from home, how do you go about cutting through the crowd of other candidates and shining when you apply and interview? Take a look at chapter 4 to find out.

FOUR

How to Land the Perfect Work-from-Home Job

You cannot make working from home happen without relying on today's virtual tools—and the same is true of a job search. In fact, the Internet, and to a lesser extent your e-mail and telephone, may be the tools you'll use to seek work and possibly even interview for and accept a position. When you are looking for a home-based job, you may never meet your employer in person. (It's always a good idea to keep networking, however. Having a pool of industry acquaintances to call on for mentoring, advice, or future jobs is a tremendous advantage.)

Regardless of how you search for the perfect position that allows you to work from home, you need a targeted résumé and cover letter that sell your strengths, the ability to nail job interviews, and some negotiating know-how.

Work Your Résumé and Application Materials

Almost without exception, you answer any job posting or rumor of an open position by submitting a résumé—or a job application that includes your résumé's carefully crafted information. Although opinions vary on how employers use the résumés they receive, what a résumé should look like, and what to include on one, you must have an up-to-date résumé.

When you are looking for a home-based job, your résumé is more crucial than ever. That's because you are no longer just competing with other job seekers in your area—your competition might even be worldwide. Also, there is a chance that you won't meet the employer face-to-face—ever—so your résumé must carry the weight of helping prospective employers choose you. The bottom line: your résumé should be as comprehensive, carefully crafted, and error-free as you can make it.

Once you have created the perfect résumé, you should continue to revise it. Every single time you apply for a job, you should review your original résumé, save it as a new document, and then revise to best match the advertised opening. This may mean changing or adding information, shifting emphasis within your work history, tweaking your summary statement, or all of the above.

Your Résumé Collection

It pays to save every version of your résumé that you create—keeping in mind that you will need to know which document you sent to which employer. Imagine that you e-mail a résumé for a terrific job posting, and two weeks—and many résumé revisions—later you are called for an in-person interview. You should bring hard copies of your résumé along, but which version matches the one you e-mailed? You'd better be able to figure it out, so that all copies match exactly.

Your Work-from-Home Résumé

As with a traditional résumé, your résumé for a work-from-home position should focus on your professional skills, experience, and accomplishments, implying what these factors can do to benefit an employer. Avoid any mention of why or how much you want to work from home—that has no place in your job search. And if the job you are applying for is explicitly home-based, you should not have to mention working from home at all. Still, it's a good idea to clarify that you are seeking to work from home with targeted key words and phrases that clarify your goals and position you for the type of job you want. Here are a few examples, for use in different sections of the résumé:

> *Career objective.* This optional section at the top of a résumé can be used to specify that you are seeking a home-based position. When you revise your résumé to match a job posting, copy the terms the employer uses, whether "telecommuter" or "remote." *Example:* "To obtain a telecommuting position that will allow me to expand my telephone customer service skills and experience." (Note the implied benefit to the employer—always stress how hiring *you* will help *them.*)
>
> *Skills summary.* Another optional section (which should not be used if you include a career objective or similar opening), a skills summary can be used to highlight your strengths—specifically, as they pertain to working from home—if you are looking for your first job or making a career transition. When you can't list strengths and skills under each previous job held, this is a good way to highlight your abilities. *Example:* "A reliable self-starter

with strong organizational skills, adept at customer service, and with great people skills."

Key traits. Either in your skills summary or sprinkled throughout your résumé, include words and phrases that describe an ideal telecommuting employee. *Examples: Disciplined, independent, self-starter, quick learner, organized, reliable.*

Key skills. It is common to include a list of skills at the bottom of your résumé, where you might name the software programs you are proficient at, the languages you are fluent in, and so on. When looking for a work-from-home job, you can assure the employer that you are ready for the position by using this section to include relevant skills. *Examples: Good time management, project management*, proficiency in digital tools you might need such as Skype and Google Docs.

Keywords: Your Key to Making the Cut

Whether you submit your résumé by e-mail or hand it to someone at a networking event, the first thing a hiring organization does is scan it—either by a human or a software program—for keywords that match the job requirements. If your résumé doesn't include enough keywords, it won't even make the first cut. And if it is scanned by software, the people who typically make yes-or-no decisions won't even lay eyes on it.

The keywords you need depend on the position you are applying for. For example, if you're applying for a position as a payroll clerk, your résumé might be scanned for the following words and phrases: *payroll, timekeeping, payroll discrepancies, verify, exemp-*

tions, earnings and deductions, compile, analyze, and the names of software programs or degrees specified in the job posting.

How do you find keywords? Definitely scan the job posting itself and use the same terminology. If the posting requires "English-Spanish translator," then use that exact term and even punctuation. The same goes for terms used in the job description, if you can find it on the organization's website or through other channels.

Other sources for finding good keywords are industry publications, the organization's website, and information on the job title in the Bureau of Labor Statistics' *Occupational Outlook Handbook.* Do a little research and start compiling a list of keywords that you can use to strengthen your résumé, your cover letter, and your job interviews.

Tips on Sending Your Résumé

It is common practice these days to submit your résumé by e-mail or through an employer's website or to fill out an online application for a job. When submitting your résumé, make sure you follow the employer's requirements. Double-check details on how the employer requires or requests replies, including types of attachments. Different companies may prefer PDFs over Microsoft Word documents (or vice versa), may reject any compressed files such as Zip files, or may disallow any attachments at all. If there are no restrictions on file types, it is best to send a PDF of your résumé. That way, you don't have to worry about software incompatibility, and your document can't be inadvertently changed by someone else.

If you can't find any requirements for résumé submission, in addition to an attached PDF it is wise to copy and paste a plain-text version of your résumé—one that has all formatting and special characters stripped out—into the body of your e-mail, just in case attachments are blocked. You might do this even if an attachment is requested, in order to be doubly sure your résumé reaches the reader.

When you do attach a résumé, make sure you name the document so that it is easily identifiable. Your best bet is "yourlast name_resume.doc"—and be sure to include the extension .doc or .pdf so that it can be opened easily.

A final word on e-mailing your résumé in response to a job opening: choose your subject line carefully. Write a line that makes it clear what your e-mail is in response to and even sells you a little. Include the job title or code used in the posting. If you are sending an unsolicited résumé, make the subject line a descriptor of you: "Database manager with 12 years' experience," or "Physical therapist seeks challenging opportunity."

Tips on Completing Online Job Applications

Many job boards (including Careerbuilder.com and Monster.com), temp agencies, and recruiters require an online application for any position, and individual employers may use this tool as a first step as well. To ensure that you complete these online forms with carefully chosen language (including keywords) and without typos or errors, try this efficient process:

1. Save the most applicable version of your résumé for the position and strip out all formatting, including boldface, italics, bullet points, and centering. Use one typeface and size—preferably something commonly used like Times or Arial.
2. Remove columns or tabbed sections.

3. Remove any hard returns at the end of lines.

4. Save your document as a text file with the extension .txt to ensure that all invisible coding is stripped out. Review the resulting document using a text editor program such as Notepad or SimpleText to be sure you are seeing it accurately.

5. Use this final document to copy and paste sections of your résumé into appropriate form fields.

6. Proofread every field you have filled in before you click "complete" on any online form.

Cover Your Bases with a Great Cover Letter

Not all employers value cover letters, but these additional documents are a great way to enhance your résumé and move it to the top of the stack. As with your résumé, start with one cover letter and then write or revise a new version for each job posting you apply for. Use the letter to

▸ Show off the knowledge of the company or industry that you gained through research

▸ Highlight one of your specific skills or experiences that is an ideal match for this opening

▸ Reinforce why you are well suited to work from home, emphasizing key skills and personality traits

▸ Explain—briefly and with a positive spin—any red flags in your résumé, such as a long gap in employment

▸ Demonstrate your communication skills with a well-written letter

If you are e-mailing your résumé, the body of your e-mail message should act as your cover letter. But don't treat it as a typical e-mail. Write a business letter with a salutation ("Dear Human Resources Manager," for example), paragraphs, and a sign-off ("Sincerely yours," followed by your full name). Drafting the complete letter in a word processing document allows you to edit, proofread, spell-check, and save it before copying it into e-mail. And this way you can save and find previous letters to revise as you apply for each new position.

How to Handle Salary Requirements

If a job posting states that salary requirement or salary history is required, pay attention. Countless hirers and recruiters have said that, if they ask for this and don't see it, the résumé doesn't make the cut. Your cover letter is the ideal place for this. To give yourself the most flexibility, give the most general information.

Your salary history might read something like this: "I started my last position with an annual salary of $43,000, and when I left I was earning $46,500."

Your salary requirements might state: "I am looking for a position that offers a salary in the range of $43,000 to $50,000."

You will, of course, do your salary research before you state any requirements so that your expectations are realistic.

Ace Your Interviews

Landing an interview is cause for celebration—you made the cut. Take a moment to congratulate yourself, and then start preparing. It is likely that all interviews for a home-based job will be done over the phone, but the same steps for successful interviewing apply: preparation, research, careful consideration, and practice.

Know it all. When scheduling any type of interview, make sure you get all the details, including where and when the interview is (including whom to ask for when you arrive for an in-person interview), the names and job titles of everyone you'll be speaking with, an estimated time frame (will it take one hour or all afternoon?), and whether you will be expected to take any assessment, skills, or software tests.

Research the organization. Read the organization's website thoroughly, and do an Internet search to see what else you can learn about current and recent events—including annual reports and changes in the company's stock (if it is publicly traded). If you know any current or past employees, request a quick phone conversation to get the inside scoop. Organize the facts you gather and consider how to use them in the interview—perhaps as questions about recent developments, or to highlight a point or two.

Think it through. Be prepared to sell yourself—your skills, experience, successes, and innate talents. Make a list of your strongest selling points and give careful thought to how to work each into conversation. Ideally, you will have a chance to tell a story about a problem you solved, a specific accomplishment that demonstrates a relevant skill, or even a lesson you learned. Practice telling your stories concisely.

Practice makes perfect. Ask a friend to play the part of the interviewer, even if you have to supply the questions. This can reduce your nervousness and build your confidence. You can also try rehearsing your stories and other answers in front of a mirror, or even videotape yourself. Check your body language. Do you look engaged and interested? Try leaning forward, keeping an open expression on your face, and uncrossing your arms. Even if you are interviewing over the phone, your body language will influence how you convey your interest and attitude.

Keep in mind that as a home-based employee your telephone skills are particularly important. You might want to add telephone practice to this step; call a friend and ask her to give you some honest feedback on your telephone voice and manners before your interview.

Interviewing over the Phone

Even if the employer is located in your area, you are likely to have at least one interview by phone. This is more time-efficient for the interviewer (and you, too). Sometimes these calls are used to screen multiple candidates and weed out those who don't meet all requirements. Even if this is the case, treat your phone appointment like any other first interview and be prepared before you pick up the phone.

Consider where and when you'll be on the call. Ideally you'll be in your home office; if this is not an option, find another quiet spot where you won't be interrupted. If your mobile phone does not get excellent reception there, ask the interviewer to call you on a landline, or find a different place.

Have some notes or even an outline ready to refer to, along with a copy of your résumé, to ensure that you get to tell your prepared stories. And, as with an in-person interview, take an active part in the conversation. Ask questions to demonstrate your intelligence and personality and to show off your knowledge of the organization. Keep your answers concise, but try to elaborate on everything rather than giving a short "yes" or "no."

Webcam Interviews

Job interviews via computerized video chats are growing in popularity—especially for interstate interviews. In "How Skype Is Changing the Job Interview," Barbara Kiviat offers pointers for preparing yourself and your backdrop to appear on-screen. Check it out on the *Time* magazine website, www.time.com/time/magazine.

Whether you are interviewing over the phone or in person, put yourself in control from the start of the conversation. Begin by asking the interviewer for a brief overview of the open position. The more you learn about the position, department, and organization, the better you can tailor your comments to demonstrate what a great fit you are.

Many people have trouble talking about themselves and their successes. Some simply don't do well under pressure. That's why it is crucial to practice not just *what* you want to say but *how* you say it—speaking clearly and without rushing, not talking too much, and using eye contact and positive body language.

If you are lucky enough to be called back for a second interview, keep in mind that one thing the employer will be looking for is whether you are a good fit for the culture of the company. The questioning may be more personal: What would you do in this situation? How do you handle conflict? What types of activities do you enjoy in your off-hours? Be sure to ask more questions in this interview; you want to have the information you need to make a decision if you are offered the job.

Before You Say Good-bye

There are two things you should cover at the end of every interview:

1. Let the interviewer know that you are interested in the job. State clearly and directly that you want the position.
2. Ask what the interview process is and how it's going. It is perfectly acceptable to inquire about next steps and when you should expect to hear about them. You can also ask how many other candidates are being interviewed and where you stand after the interview.

Pop Quizzes

Many organizations use tests to help qualify job candidates. During the interview process, you may be asked to take one or more of the following:

Assessment test. Typically multiple-choice in format, these tests are designed to reveal your personal characteristics and values, which lets the hirer know whether you are ethical and honest or whether you are a good match for their corporate culture.

Skills test. Depending on the job, you may be tested on knowledge of a specific software program, math abilities, or even judgment.

Typing test. How many words per minute can you type?

Drug test. If the company requires drug screening, you may need to pass a drug test as a last step in the employment process.

Ask about any tests before the interview, so that you know what you'll be expected to do and when.

Following Up

After each interview, there are a few tasks you should take care of immediately:

> *Jot down some notes.* Before you forget anything, write down your impressions of the company, the job, and the interviewers for your own future reference. Make sure you have the names and titles of everyone you spoke to.
>
> *Contact references.* If the organization asked for professional or personal references, contact those individuals immediately to notify them. If appropriate, remind them or coach them on what to emphasize about you.
>
> *Write thank-yous.* Write, type, or e-mail a personal thank-you note to each person you interviewed with.
>
> *Check in.* If you don't hear back from the interviewer, it is okay to contact the company. If you were told that the hiring decision should be made within two weeks, contact the company a couple of days before that estimated deadline. If you don't know the time frame, wait about a week before making contact.

Timing the Money Talk

Don't jump the gun naming your salary requirements. Although the topic of money may come up early—as a request for your salary history or requirements, for instance—the standard rule is, don't bring up this topic until the employer makes you a job offer. That initial request for information was not part of salary negotiation or discussion; they simply wanted to see if you were in the general range they would be offering.

You should start your second interview with the information you need to negotiate your salary and other terms. Not all employers act this fast, but you must be prepared in case they do so that you can negotiate with confidence. Whether an offer is made then and there, in a follow-up phone call, or during a subsequent interview, remember this: once the opportunity for negotiating the terms of your new job has passed, you'll never be able to make up the difference between what you get and what you could have had. So always negotiate for the best possible package.

Negotiate Like a Pro

Nervous about negotiating? Don't be. Employers and human resource professionals *expect* you to negotiate their job offers. Typically, the first offer of pay and benefits is not set in stone. Rather, it is a starting point, and you should reach higher.

It is a good tactic to let the company negotiator begin the conversation. This ensures that this is in fact the right time to negotiate—and you hold the advantage if the employer names a figure first, which is something you should try to get the negotiator to do.

If you are asked what you expect or want, dodge the question for the moment by asking if there is a set salary range. If the salary range offered matches your research, negotiate for the high end of the range, reminding the interviewer of your strengths, skills, and experience.

If you are put in the position of stating your figure first, give a pay range that you base on your own research, and name your sources. It is important that you begin your negotiation with a solid grasp of what is realistic in terms of pay, benefits, and perks for the type of job you've been offered. Before you enter this negotiation, study sources like Salary.com, PayScale.com, professional association websites, and JobStar.org to get current information. And be sure you understand where you fit in the range of experience, skills, and value for position.

If the employer's first offer or salary range seems too low, acknowledge that the organization has a set salary range for this position, but make a case for increasing that range in the present circumstances. Point out your salary sources and the industry averages. (Don't use your own previous or current salary as an example.) Remind your interviewer of several of your top selling points, illustrating why you are a valuable candidate.

If negotiations reach a point where the final salary offer is still low, divert the conversation to more or better benefits. Remember: It's the complete package of salary and benefits that count, and just about everything is negotiable:

> ▸ home office resources such as Internet, phone, fax, office supplies
> ▸ flextime
> ▸ health insurance (If you are already covered by your spouse, or by the military, can you negotiate a higher salary instead of health coverage?)
> ▸ vacation time
> ▸ timing first salary review (Negotiate it earlier, in hopes of getting your first raise sooner.)
> ▸ retirement plans
> ▸ bonus plans
> ▸ tuition reimbursement
> ▸ stock options
> ▸ signing bonus
> ▸ start date

If a final offer is made, it is acceptable (even advisable) to ask for time to consider it before accepting—but no more than a day or two.

If, in the end, you can't get a package that suits your needs or wants, end the interview politely but try to leave the door open in case the organization's decision makers change their minds. After interviewing other candidates, they may find that you were worth what you wanted after all.

Home-Based Work: Worth More or Less?

When you are researching salaries for a position, do you need to distinguish between working from home and working in a company office? The answer is "sometimes." If you are interviewing for a position with an organization that hires both home-based and on-site employees for the same job, all positions should have the same pay ranges. However, if the job you want is home-based only with this organization, you may see some differences in pay rates.

One school of thought is that home-based positions should pay more. After all, the employer is saving money by not providing workspace and other resources. The higher pay makes up for what you spend on office resources. Alternatively, your employer might pay directly for expenses such as high-speed Internet or a dedicated mobile phone for your work.

However, before you start ratcheting up your required pay range, be aware of another school of thought: many employers are aware of the value that working at home holds for people, and they know they can leverage this preference. According to a 2011 survey by Dice Holdings, 35 percent of technology professionals said they would take up to 10 percent less pay to telecommute full time. Consequently, organizations may actually pay lower rates to home-based workers.

Final Step: Accepting the Offer

Once you and your future employer have settled on your salary and benefits package, follow up with an immediate e-mail that restates the agreement. In that message, do the following:

> ▸ Acknowledge the offer and thank the employer for it.
> ▸ Clearly state the terms of the offer as you understand them and ask for confirmation of those terms.
> ▸ Request some time to consider. You want to review the job, the salary, and everything that goes with it.
> ▸ Find out whom you should contact with your final decision. It may be the human resources person or the hiring manager.
> ▸ Once you have considered the job and what it entails, matched the offered pay to your budget, and taken whatever steps you need to make sure this job will work for you, call *and* e-mail your assigned contact with an enthusiastic acceptance.

Or, Rejecting the Offer

What if you decide you don't want the job? If that's the case, do the right thing: Call the hiring manager or human resources professional to let him know your decision. Then follow up right away with an e-mail to that person, thanking all involved for their time and consideration and restating that you are declining the offer. If appropriate, give your reasons for declining—you are taking another position, or you could not reach agreement on salary or benefits. Be sure to keep your tone professional and courteous. Don't burn any bridges.

Your next step: making sure you excel in your new job in spite of the challenges, distractions, and differences of working from your home. Chapter 5 tells how.

FIVE

Making It Work

Once you land your first home-based job, you enter a unique world of work. Starting any new position is challenging and often disorienting; doing so when you're the only one in the room is even more so. For advice on what it takes to adapt and excel in this situation, we asked a couple of experts who recruit and advise telecommuters and their managers. Corinne Miller is the principal and founder of Innovating Results!, a consulting company that specializes in training managers with telecommuting employees. Herb Cogliano is CEO of Sullivan & Cogliano, a national IT contract staffing company based in Boston that matches contractors to telecommuting and on-site positions.[1]

Cogliano points out that employees and contractors must demonstrate their commitment to the job: "When someone is working from home, we look at their level of motivation, professionalism, and maturity. If that person has a dog barking loudly in the background when they're on the phone, or if they are living with an aging parent [who needs care], they're setting themselves up to fail."

Miller warns that, when you start working from home, it isn't safe to rely on your manager to set the expectations and process: "Telecommuters expect their boss to do all the right things for managing them, but you can't count on this. For example, you should be checking in at least once a week on a formally scheduled call or web conference. If your manager doesn't arrange this, take the initiative to set it up yourself. Make it easy for your manager to connect."

This chapter reviews the key components you need for becoming a work-from-home star, based in part on insights from these two telecommuting experts.

Communicate

The top factor in making a telecommuting arrangement work is strong communication skills—both written and verbal. This starts with Corinne Miller's point about being proactive in communicating with your manager. You need to communicate a great deal when you are starting out, to make sure that you understand your manager's expectations, your work processes, and your goals. You even have to be a good enough communicator to ferret out what no one thinks to communicate.

Employers that have formal telecommuting programs are likely to have communication procedures in place, though these may not target all of your needs. Employers that are not accustomed to telecommuting workers require even sharper communication skills from those workers to ensure success. In either case, be proactive about getting information you need, and watch for ways to improve existing communication procedures. Start with the basics: "Processes are not typically formalized, so you'd better be really clear in getting this information," Miller stresses. "Processes that involve hard copies should be made electronic if possible" so that you stay in the loop.

Tips for Good Communication

Here are some ground rules for keeping the lines of communication open—particularly when you are working from home with a manager and colleagues who are all at company sites.

Think on your feet, and ask questions. In any conversation, whether online or on the phone, be alert for missing or unclear information, explanations you don't understand, or unfamiliar concepts. Then ask for clarifications. If you aren't able to ask immediately, write yourself a note to get the information as soon as possible.

Listen up. Communication involves more than talking. Listen closely when you're on the phone, even in the most boring conference call. Inattentiveness can lead to forgetting what you did hear, and the less often you have to contact someone for answers you should already have, the better. Also, pay attention to voice inflections so that you can gauge others' moods and personalities.

Take notes. Particularly in a new job, you're going to have a lot of information to process and remember. And that's more difficult when you're working alone. Organize your notes on every conversation and meeting so that you can review information whenever necessary. If you keep your notes electronically, you can search them quickly and easily when a question comes up.

Look for patterns. Watch for the gaps that occur in communications. Is there a pattern, such as one person in particular who forgets to invite you to meetings? Or one specific project for which you always seem to miss communications? When you see a hole like this, figure out who can change the situation (if you can't take care of it yourself) and how to approach that person.

Be flexible. Ask your boss, other managers, and hard-to-reach colleagues about their preferred means of communication, and use those means—but be aware of other options. Your busy new boss may stress that e-mail is the best way to reach her, but suppose you find that she is not responding to messages quickly enough for you to do your job efficiently. If you have an immediate need or question, try picking up the phone or instant messaging her to see if you can get a faster response. Then note what really works best.

Make a friend. Sometimes gossip is good. Make a friend on the "inside" who can tell you about the informal things that come up. It is invaluable to know if someone rolled his eyes while you were pitching your idea over the phone in a group meeting, or the latest rumors about reorganization that are making the rounds.

Sum up. Take a moment at the end of each day to review your communications, both good and bad. What did you accomplish that your boss needs to know about? The rest of your team? Review e-mails, notes, and any other communications and consider carefully who needs to know what. Similarly, did you get any hints that you are missing information?

Strategize. As you learn your job and get comfortable working from home, you can set up your own processes to keep communication open. These may be private, such as typing up your notes, or they may be ways to stay in touch with coworkers: weekly calls, shared calendars, project management applications, or Google Docs, for example.

Make Connections to Others

If you never meet your colleagues face-to-face, it is especially important to get to know them. Go beyond the list of names and job titles, and try to ascertain the strengths and knowledge of those you'll be working with and relying on regularly. That way, you know whom to approach when you need specific information.

In a new job, you can be proactive with this. After discussing with your manager, plan to call appropriate individuals to introduce yourself or say hello. Tell each a little bit about yourself, and ask about them. Each call can take as little as three minutes if either of you is very busy. Include support people within the company, such as the receptionist, IT help, and human resources.

Corinne Miller points out that "if most of your colleagues are in the office, they're connecting with each other constantly. You have to plan your serendipity and be a little bit more aware and purposeful in contacting them in order to maintain a relationship."

When you speak (or communicate electronically) with coworkers, try to find—or build—some common ground. Your goal is to demonstrate that you are a real person, even if they'll never see your face. Create a private joke, commiserate over a tough project, or congratulate them on small successes—and if you are relying on someone to be your "eyes and ears" on the ground, try to reciprocate with small favors so that the relationship isn't a one-way street.

Phone Friends

When forming relationships with your coworkers over the phone, follow these tips to help you stay popular among your peers:

Be brief but friendly. Everyone is overworked these days, so keep phone calls quick. But don't be too abrupt. Remember to start the call with a warm greeting and end with your thanks.

Be positive. Keep your voice and your attitude cheerful and positive, and your colleagues will be more likely to welcome your calls.

Don't wear out your welcome. If you have a lot of questions, thus creating a lot of phone calls, avoid calling the same person over and over. Sally in the accounting department may be very friendly, but that doesn't mean she is truly happy to hear from you three times day. If others can give you answers, spread the wealth, and give Sally a break.

One downside of telecommuting is that you are literally left out of things—particularly if telecommuters are in the minority of employees at your organization. And this goes for more than just birthday cakes; you may be "out of sight, out of mind" when it comes to new opportunities. This means that it is crucial that you work on keeping relationships strong and making your presence felt.

> "There is a long-term disadvantage associated with working from home related to lack of face time with the managers and the likelihood that I will not advance because I am not in proximity with the rest of the team."
>
> —*Diana Wellington, marketing manager*

Solve Your Own Problems ···

One of the toughest aspects of working from home is the forced independence. No matter how well this might suit you, there are occasions when you'll wish you could turn to the worker in the next cubicle to ask a question—but there's no next cubicle. So you'd better either be prepared to figure out the problem yourself or know whom to ask. Corinne Miller says she values "tenaciousness in problem solving" in telecommuting employees.

Because in a new position you are likely to be asking a lot of questions, it is best to try to do things yourself when you can. You seem a lot more professional and just plain competent if you can remember how to access your computer's remote desktop yourself rather than calling the IT department several times a day.

How do you become a good problem solver? These tips can get you started:

> *Make sure you have all available information.* When you start a new job or a new project, try to gather as many resources as your employer has to offer, including manuals, web pages, and orientation materials. Be careful in filing information, and keep track of what you have so that you know where to look for answers when a problem arises months later.
>
> *Trust your abilities.* You should have an idea of the types of problems you are able to tackle. For example, you may be an accomplished researcher, which can help with a lot of challenges, but have trouble grasping how some technology works, which may result in multiple calls to the help desk. Regardless of your skills, play to them. If you excel at research, you may be able to research your way to success, even with a technical issue.

Exercise good judgment. You have to use your own
judgment to decide whether it is better to spend extra
time searching for an answer on your own or ask for
help. If you manage to solve a problem without asking
for help, but it takes you six hours, then that probably is
not a productive use of your time.

Project Professionalism

In chapter 2 we covered the importance of setting up an appropriate
workspace. Not only is this important to you for your comfort and
convenience, it's important to your employer. Herb Cogliano says,
"The best [telecommuters] have designated the right space for their
work, they have the right equipment . . . and they have created an
environment that is organized and has the privacy that allows them
to concentrate on their job."

Depending on the level and type of job, your employer may
require you and your home office setup to adhere to strict gover-
nance, including security and compliance protocols and procedures
and protection of confidential or proprietary information. Cogliano
warns that your employer may even require a home visit to check
on your workspace before hiring you—in some instances, as a
surprise visit.

Although your employer may provide you with equipment or
reimburse you for certain expenses such as high-speed Internet, it
is up to you to ensure that you have providers that will maintain
uninterrupted service. "You must be equipped to communicate
effectively, and to do your job. This might include e-mail and
[instant messaging], file sharing systems, phone and conferencing
capabilities, and other tools," stresses Corinne Miller.

Deliver Results

The ultimate indication that you are succeeding while working from home is your productivity. If you are getting your job done and meeting or exceeding your employer's expectations, you are a work-from-home success story. The problem is, you have to understand exactly what those expectations or goals are. It is essential that you and your manager each know the goals associated with your job.

This information may be included in the job description or covered in your orientation (and any subsequent performance reviews). If it is not, or if you do not clearly understand the goals outlined, then it is vital that you arrange a conversation with your manager within your first week of employment to clarify these expectations. If this conversation is necessary, then put the goals in writing and e-mail them to your manager to confirm, so that you are both literally working off the same page.

As Corinne Miller suggests, "Make sure your goals are well defined—this includes behavioral goals or expectations. When nonverbal communication is taken away, clarity of communication suffers, so ask questions to ensure you understand your manager's expectations, including when and how you will join impromptu meetings."

Having short- and long-term expectations in writing spells out whether you are doing your job correctly. Keep a list of goals or expectations where you can see it, and take stock regularly to consider whether you're doing a good job. If you feel you are not meeting the necessary goals, give your work performance some careful consideration. Are you having trouble staying on task because you are working from home? If so, what exactly is the problem, and can you fix it easily? For example, if your children are continually distracting you, then make arrangements that will give you uninterrupted work time. If, however, you are struggling with the work itself, that's a more serious matter. You may need to ask for guidance or mentoring, take some of your own time to master your new responsibilities, or take stock of your abilities and knowledge.

You may think you are doing well, but it's a good idea to ask your manager for a performance review one or two months into the job. Ask for feedback on any areas that might need improvement. Then work with that feedback in mind.

"Your manager will know it's not working when goals aren't being met: the work isn't being done on time, with quality," says Miller. And if you are struggling with the solitude of working alone, that might become clear to your manager, as well as to yourself: "The manager might see behaviors change. If the person stops participating in meetings and gets quiet, they might be depressed. Also, the manager may start hearing complaints about the person from peers or customers."

If you are having problems with the job, your employer should give you an opportunity to improve—so make the most of that opportunity, and use it to figure out quickly how to do better so that you can continue to work from home.

Calling It Quits

If, after a trial period, it seems that your work-from-home position is just not working for you, it's time to ask yourself some tough questions:

▸ Is there anything you can do to improve the situation? If the writing is on the wall and you're released from the job (or give your resignation), leave on good terms.

▸ If the problem lies with working from home, would you be willing to do the same job on-site? If your employer is willing, is that feasible for you?

▸ Are you still interested in pursuing a work-from-home job for your next employment opportunity? If so, what can you do differently to ensure that you will succeed next time? How can you put what you've learned to good use?

As with any job, starting a new telecommuting position comes with special challenges and a steep learning curve. But if with time you get comfortable with your duties and responsibilities, and perfect your workspace along with your communication skills and the other traits of a good telecommuter, you will discover for yourself the joys of working from home.

Note

1. Comments in this chapter from Corinne Miller and Herb Cogliano taken from telephone interviews with the author, December 2 and 9, 2011.

Part III

Working for Yourself from Home

SIX

The Fundamentals of Self-Employment

Working from home as your own boss is very different from being a telecommuter employed by an organization. In fact, the only thing the two have in common is the "at home" aspect. Working for yourself means you are the boss, the bookkeeper, the marketing department, the administrative assistant, and the one who does all the work. You are solely responsible for earning the income and providing the benefits you need to get by.

On top of this, you can choose working for yourself for a variety of different goals. Do you want to start a side business that allows you to earn extra money? Do the work you love? Or lay the groundwork for an eventual full-time business? Do you want to become a freelance worker, replacing your traditional job with self-employment? Do you want to work from home as a temp worker or contractor, completing projects under short- or long-term contracts with an agency or employer?

Whichever path you choose in working for yourself, the fundamentals outlined in this chapter apply. Even if your new side business of selling items on eBay nets you little more than your home office expenses at first, you should still follow these guidelines for paying income tax and consider the other recommendations and options outlined here.

> Brandi Weiss is a hair stylist who works in a professional salon but also has a station in her basement at home, where she's worked on the side for more than ten years.
>
> "It's more convenient for me because I don't have a commute, I don't have to worry about parking, and I don't have to get dressed up. I can set my own hours, and I choose my customers. The downside is that I have people coming in my house all the time—I don't really like that. And people call my home phone all the time. They think I'm open twenty-four hours."

Pros and Cons of Working for Yourself

In chapter 2 we listed some pros and cons of working from home. Of course, these apply to those who work for themselves from home too. But there are additional factors to consider when you are self-employed, most of them two-edged swords:

> ▸ You can be your own boss, *but* you may find that you don't want the added responsibility and work.
> ▸ There is potential for earning more money, *but* you have no guaranteed income from month to month and no employer-sponsored benefits.
> ▸ Your are free to set your own schedule and accept the projects you like, *but* the need for income may force you to accept work you don't want.

▶ Self-employment may be the only way to do what you love and be creative, *but* what you love may not be as enjoyable when it is your employment.

▶ You get to work from home, *but* home-based work is even more isolating for the self-employed.

There is excitement and risk in going on your own, *but* you are responsible for all aspects of your business, from fixing computer problems to collecting payments.

> "Since I started working for myself, I have more flexibility with my time. In my previous full-time job I did not have much time to relax, and I have been able to spend more time doing personal things. Also, I can choose what I would like to work on. I like to work on international projects, so I strive to be involved in these types of projects."
>
> —*Mauricio Gutierrez, senior airport planner/engineer*

Basic Forms of Business

When you decide to work for yourself from home, you are starting up a business. Even if you decide to earn some spending money by posting your artwork on Etsy.com, you are now a business—no matter how informal. Depending on how you plan to proceed, this is the time to consider whether or how to formalize your business.

Sole Proprietorship

Most people starting a home-based business become sole proprietors. This is the simplest, most basic business structure, and it requires no registration or legal fees. It simply means that you are a one-person business and that you are solely responsible for all assets and liabilities of your work.

The biggest drawback to a sole proprietorship is liability. If your business incurs debt or a lawsuit, you are personally responsible; your savings, home, and possessions are on the line. Consider how serious these risks are for the type of work you want to do. If you are caring for people's pets, you'll be responsible for possessing house keys or access codes as well as the safety of the animals (and other people the animals encounter). You are at higher risk of getting sued in this business than someone who enters data from his home computer, and you need to think about protecting your assets.

As a sole proprietor, all money you make is taxed as personal income. You simply file income tax as an individual (or married couple)—but with more forms involved. And if your business grows, you can legally hire employees or contract with other freelancers to help out.

Limited Liability Corporation

Incorporating your business as a limited liability corporation (LLC) protects your personal assets. If your business is an LLC and you get sued by a client, or your business goes bankrupt, it is your business assets at risk—not your personal assets.

If you form a one-person LLC, you pay taxes just as if you were a sole proprietor, including paying self-employment taxes on your income. If your LLC has multiple owners, paying taxes becomes more complicated. Alternatively, you can identify yourself as an employee of your LLC (rather than the owner) and give yourself a salary, in which case your income (of $10,000 or more) is subject to income tax withholding as well as self-employment taxes.

How to Set Up an LLC

Fill out and file a simple form called Articles of Organization with your secretary of state's office (or a similar entity). You may need to pay a fee when you file. Only after you have registered your LLC should you apply for any business licenses or permits that may be required in your locality.

Partnership

If you are starting a business with one or more other people, you may choose to register the business as a general partnership, a limited partnership, or a joint venture (as well as an LLC with multiple owners). A general partnership is much like a sole proprietorship except that it obviously encompasses more than one person. All partners report their share of income and losses on their individual tax returns.

In a limited partnership, one or more partners run the business while the "limited" partner or partners act only as investors and are not personally liable for the business debts.

How to Set Up a Partnership

Whichever type of partnership you establish, it is essential that you formalize the business arrangement, clarifying in writing how you will split business responsibilities, profits (or losses), and liabilities as well as the duration of the agreement. You should hire an attorney to help set up the partnership, or at the very least you should create and sign a written agreement that outlines these factors.

Corporation

Setting up a corporate entity is probably beyond the scope of anyone who picked up this book looking for a way to earn money from home. But, for the record, a corporation is chartered by the state in which it is headquartered, is run by stockholders (who have limited liability), is legally bound to hold annual shareholder meetings, and files corporate taxes. The Small Business Administration website (www.sba.gov) provides details on the different types of corporations and the benefits of each.

How to Set Up a Corporation
You file specific forms and pay fees to your secretary of state office or state corporations commission.

Nonprofit Organization

It is possible to start a home-based nonprofit entity such as a charity, a trade association, or a political group. You must, however, keep in mind that these organizations follow strict laws and guidelines, including having a board of directors. This board makes decisions and sets policies, including the salary and benefits you draw from the organization. You also need to file articles of incorporation with your state, draft bylaws, and apply for nonprofit status from the IRS. For more information on starting a nonprofit, visit the website of the Society for Nonprofit Organizations at www.snpo.org.

Franchise

When you purchase a home-based franchise, you acquire ready-made identity, support, and structure. These businesses, such as

Jani-King commercial cleaning services and WSI Internet online marketing solutions, work just like Quiznos, Curves, and other traditional storefront franchises. You sign a long-term contract with the parent company and pay a hefty franchise fee to get started. Depending on the type of business you have, you have additional operating expenses and you pay royalty fees to your parent company.

Before signing a franchise agreement, review the full disclosure of information that the parent company is legally obligated to give you and consult an attorney who has experience with franchises.

Naming Your Business

Entire books are devoted to the art and science of choosing a name for your business that is attractive, appropriate, and effective. You should definitely put careful thought into the name you use—including the option of simply using the name your parents gave you.

Once you've come up with a business name you like, verify that it is available. You don't have to select a name that has never been used, but avoid duplicating or coming close to duplicating the name of a similar business. You cannot use the name of a business already registered in your county—or, in the case of LLCs, in your state—and you should avoid anything that sounds like a major brand such as McDonald's, which has sued companies over their names. Your county clerk's office can search a database of business names (including unregistered trademarks) currently in use in your region or state. You can also do your own online search on your potential business name and check ThomasNet.com for unregistered trademark names of companies and brands.

If your preferred business name is available, file it with your state government—or in some cases your county government. Sole proprietors and partnerships must file their trade names, or DBAs for "doing business as," with an appropriate agency within their state or county. There is typically a small fee for this.[1] Filing the name of a new LLC is part of the process of registering the corporation; separate DBA filing is not necessary.

If you have a limited liability corporation, your business name must include "LLC," or "Limited Liability Corporation."

If you are a sole proprietor, you can use your personal name or come up with a business name such as ABC Tutoring or Hand E. Man Services. In either case, your personal name is the *legal* name of your business and should be used on income tax forms and other official forms and applications.

Purchasing an Existing Business

If you want to own a business but are not interested in the risk (some would say excitement) and hard work of starting from scratch, you might consider buying or taking over an existing small business. This should minimize risk—but only if you do your homework and make sure you're getting a fair deal.

Of course, the first hurdle is selecting the business you want to assume. Maybe a friend or family member started his own home-based business but no longer wants to continue, or maybe you've run across something in the news or heard about through the grapevine that sounds like a good investment. Make sure the business suits your interests, talents and skills, abilities, and budget. You won't have the luxury of shaping this business, or your clients' expectations, as you would if you were building it from the ground up—so acquire a thorough understanding of what it will take, from time commitment to cash, to keep the business going and make it a success.

Before you sign on the dotted line to acquire a business, perform your due diligence, including obtaining any necessary permits and licenses, reviewing documentation from the seller, including evidence that the business is in good standing, and drawing up a specific, legally sound sales agreement.

To determine a fair purchase price of the business, you and the seller should analyze several years of the business's operations, if possible, as well as the current competition and economy and the outlook for the industry.

The Small Business Administration offers precise advice for following these steps on its website at www.sba.gov.

Setting Up a Business Bank Account

Part of starting your own home-based business should be setting up a separate checking account (and perhaps other bank accounts) solely for your business. This is true for every type of business, including sole proprietorships. Separate accounts make it easy for you to track your business finances and help prove to clients as well as IRS auditors that you are running a business, not a hobby.

If you are happy with the bank you use for personal services, it is best to open a new business account there; that way you can easily transfer funds between accounts if necessary. But first, ask about fees associated with opening a small business account. If this additional account would be too costly, start shopping around at other banks.

If you filed a DBA name for your business, set up a bank account that accepts that name. That way, when clients pay with checks made out to Ace Accounting Services rather than to you personally, you can deposit or cash them. Simply bring in certified copies of your DBA or incorporation documentation as well as personal identification when you set up the account.

A Whole New World of Income Tax

Regardless of which type of business you establish, you are about to enter a new world of taxation. In your first year of self-employment you may need an accountant or, at the very least, some tax preparation software and a lot of self-study, to ensure that you are complying with the IRS. There are a few tax basics you should be aware of from the outset:

Self-Employment Tax
If you earn at least $400 from your business, you must pay self-employment tax and file Schedule SE (Form 1040). If you are a sole proprietor or independent contractor, you generally use Schedule C or C-EZ to figure net earnings from self-employment.

In 2011, the self-employment tax rate was 13.3 percent; this is paid in addition to your personal income tax. This deduction is your contribution to Medicare and Social Security, and if you were working for a corporation that year your employer would deduct 5.65 percent from each of your paychecks and then contribute 7.65 percent. Because you are self-employed, you are paying both the employee's and the employer's contributions.

Estimated Taxes
The good news (or perhaps the bad news) is that your self-employment tax is not paid in one lump sum. All self-employed people (including sole proprietors, LLCs, and partnerships) pay

this tax on a set schedule throughout the year. If you are earning income, you are required to pay estimated self-employment taxes in January, April, June, and September every year. The IRS charges a penalty for not paying these, or for not paying enough. And even if you pay your estimated taxes correctly, you may still end up paying more on April 15, to make up for any difference between your estimates and reality.

Your state may also require quarterly tax payments; check your state's website to find out, or consult an accountant.

Claiming Income

If you are operating your business on the up-and-up, you bill your customers for your work and, if an organization pays you more than $600 during the calendar year, it will send you a 1099-Miscellaneous form showing the total amount it paid you. You must report this income to the IRS; the customer-organization is also filing taxes, and your income from them is on record with the IRS.

Keep careful records of the compensation you receive throughout the year, and compare your total with the 1099s you receive from clients—you don't want to pay taxes on money you never earned, and you don't want to underreport your earnings.

A Self-Employed Employer

If you employ others, you must issue a 1099-Miscellaneous form for each employee. Plus, if you are an employer, operate as a corporation or partnership, or collect sales tax, you need an employer identification number, or EIN, from the IRS. Visit www .irs.gov to apply online or get more information. For simpler types of businesses, you can use your Social Security number as your EIN.

Deductions

If you are still wincing from reading about self-employment tax, this should make you feel a little better: the IRS allows you to deduct half of your self-employment tax when figuring your adjusted gross income. That's a sizable deduction, and just the start of what you can potentially deduct.

Beginning in 2010, self-employed individuals can deduct costs of health insurance, potentially including all premiums for medical, dental, and qualified long-term care insurance for themselves, spouses, and dependents including children under age twenty-seven. Visit Irs.gov to see if you would qualify for the full deduction.

You can also deduct the costs of starting up your business and the costs of maintaining a home office or workspace. The guidelines for these deductions are stringent, and you should do your research on what is legal to deduct, particularly if your income is low. For example, a home office may be deductible only if the area is used exclusively for work, including administrative work for a business such as pet sitting or handyman services. If you can confidently say that this is true of the corner of the dining room where you set up a desk and filing cabinet, measure the area and calculate what percentage of your home it occupies. If it is 5 percent for example, you can potentially deduct 5 percent of your rent or mortgage and real estate taxes, homeowner's or renter's insurance, home utilities, and home repair and maintenance.

If you are self-employed, you also may be able to take deductions for advertising, car and truck expenses, commissions and fees, insurance (other than health), legal and professional services, office expenses, supplies, some taxes and licenses, utilities, and business travel, meals, and entertainment.

You can also deduct your contribution to a retirement plan—specifically a solo 401(k) or SEP IRA (Simplified Employee Pension Individual Retirement Arrangement).

Go Straight to the Source

At the IRS website you can find the invaluable "Small Business and Self-Employed Tax Center—Your Small Business Advantage." Visit ww.irs.gov/businesses/small/index.html for detailed information and the downloadable tax forms, instructions, and explanatory documents you need.

Business or Hobby?

If your business is creating and selling artwork or crafts, the IRS is particularly interested in proof that you intend to make a profit. They want to prevent individuals from deducting expenses that support their hobbies. This simply means that you must keep thorough business records that at least show the *intention* to make a profit. According to the IRS website, the IRS presumes that an activity is carried on for profit if it is profitable in at least three of the five previous tax years, including the current year.

Audits

You should be careful not to take undue advantage of the generous deductions the IRS allows the self-employed. The IRS estimated that one in six audits performed for the 2010 tax year was on a self-employed individual. The fact is that the more complicated your tax return becomes, the greater the chance of your being selected for an audit. And if the IRS finds you guilty of exaggerating your home office space, for example, you will literally pay the penalty.

Cover Your Assets: Insurance Tips ···············

When you start a business out of your home, your insurance needs change. You may need to add specific coverage for yourself (and perhaps your family), your home, and your business. Determine what types of coverage you need, try to negotiate a good price on all your insurance (including personal home and auto, life insurance, etc.) with your current agent or through a licensed insurance broker. There are several types of coverage you should consider. As the coverage recommendations table below indicates, your insurance needs depend on your line of work

Home-Based Businesses: Recommended Insurance

BUSINESS TYPE — **INSURANCE REQUIRED/RECOMMENDED**

BUSINESS TYPE	Business Property Insurance	Liability Insurance	Professional Liability Insurance	Health Insurance
Data entry professional	x			x
Pet sitter/dog walker		x		x
Photographer	x			x
Tax preparer	x	x (if clients come to home or office)	x	x
Hair stylist	x	x		x

Business Property Insurance

Does your homeowner's or renter's insurance policy cover your business equipment, supplies, and materials? Find out now, and consider this additional coverage if it doesn't. This includes not just coverage for your property against theft or disaster but business interruption insurance, which would cover ongoing expenses if your property were destroyed and liability insurance against claims of negligence.

Tax Savings

Premiums you pay for business insurance can be deducted from your income taxes each year.

Liability Insurance

If clients or prospects ever visit your property for any reason, you need this insurance. If someone slips and falls in your hallway, you (or your business) could be sued. The same goes if you are in a client's office and damage his property or injure someone. Your personal homeowner's policy likely includes some liability, but you may want to increase it and make sure it covers a work-related visit.

Professional Liability Insurance

This type of liability insurance protects against claims of professional negligence. A freelance journalist concerned about libel lawsuits might purchase this coverage, or an accountant concerned that a single mistake could impact a customer's tax legality. You might find professional liability insurance, also called errors and omissions (E and O) insurance, through professional associations.

Business Auto Insurance

If you use your car for business—delivering merchandise, for example, or traveling to client locations—you may need additional insurance coverage. The cost will depend on how much you drive, how many people use the car (and their ages and driving records), and the value of your vehicle.

Health Insurance

This is probably the most important benefit offered to traditional full-time employees. When you are self-employed, you have to research, find, and pay for your own health coverage. This is one of the toughest challenges you face when you start a full-time business from scratch. The good news is, if you are self-employed and pay for your own health insurance, these costs are tax deductible in most cases.

Don't leave yourself or family uncovered when it comes to health insurance—a sudden illness or accident can literally bankrupt you. Start your research immediately—and keep in mind that the U.S. Patient Protection and Affordable Care Act requires that everyone have some health insurance coverage by 2014.

Here are your basic options for finding a health insurance plan:

▶ If you are married or living with someone who gets health coverage through her employer, see if you can add yourself to the policy. This still costs you, but it may be cheaper and is definitely easier than finding individual coverage.

▶ If you are younger than twenty-seven, you can be included in a parent's coverage, even if you are not a dependent.

▶ Professional associations, your local chamber of commerce, and other groups you can join may offer a group policy for members. For example, the National Association for the Self-Employed (NASE) offers members health coverage, and if you are fifty or older you can join AARP (American Association of Retired People) and find coverage through your membership. There is no guarantee that these groups offer good coverage at good prices, so do your research before you sign up for one of these insurance policies.

▸ You can shop for your own individual policy through an insurance broker or online. This is expensive and can be difficult to get if your health is poor, but you can start searching at Healthcare.gov.

▸ If you have at least one employee, you can shop for a small-group health plan policy for your business. Find a reliable insurance broker who can help you decide on a policy.

▸ If you just left a job with health insurance, you can purchase COBRA coverage from your ex-employer for up to eighteen months. This is very expensive, but you may opt to do it until you find cheaper coverage. You can sign up within sixty days of leaving your job. To find out more, talk to your organization's human resources department.

Consider coupling a high-deductible health insurance plan with a health savings account (HSA), a type of dedicated bank account used only for health care costs. You deposit up to $1,500 per year, before taxes, and use that money for copays and deductibles. This saves you money on insurance and income taxes.

Disability Insurance

What happens if you get sick or injured and are unable to work? Disability insurance pays out monthly income for a limited period, or until you are able to start working again.

There are, however, problems related to purchasing disability insurance when you are self-employed. For one, it is nearly impossible to obtain it when you are just starting out, and difficult even after that. You need proof of steady earnings for an insurance broker to base your policy on.

If you do get disability insurance, you will pay premiums but may not get much benefit. If you are unable to work, you typically have to wait ninety days to start to receive benefits, and then you get only a percentage of your stated income—usually 60 percent—for a limited time. When shopping for disability insurance, you must calculate whether you can pay your expenses given these drawbacks. Is it worth the cost of your premiums?

In most cases it is difficult to prove that you are unable to work—particularly because you work from home. Some companies don't even offer policies to home-based workers.

Legal Matters

Familiarize yourself with the laws relevant to setting up or running a business from your home, starting with your homeowner's association or apartment building. Depending on the type of work you'll be doing, and how you'll be using your home, you may need to reconsider your plan for working from home if it is obvious that you would be breaking the rules.

Check your local zoning ordinances before you apply for a license for a home-based business. If you are not allowed to conduct business from your residence, your business address may be a red flag for local authorities.

Next, check state, local, and industry laws for your business (home-based or otherwise). Your state or your local government may require you to obtain a general business license—and this is in addition to any licenses or permits required by your specialized occupation.

If you start a daycare center, a catering business, a handyman service, or many other types of business, you will likely need to obtain a professional license. In some cases you are legally obligated to have a license; in others, it simply helps you compete and get clients.

If your home-based business is in a field that is not licensed, such as writing and posting social media blurbs for clients, you can likely fly under the radar of paying for any licenses or permits. However, be aware that if your local government decided to crack down on home-based businesses, you could be fined and even barred from doing business without a license.

If your business involves selling merchandise, research your state laws regarding payment of sales tax. You may be required to pay your state's sales tax directly to your state, or you may have to collect tax from customers, keep track of the money, and then pay it to the state. Visit the website of your state's department of revenue to begin your research.

If you plan to sell products (or even some services) that are subject to state sales tax, first complete and turn in an application for a state sales tax permit. Keep your permit, and stay on top of any changes to state sales tax laws through your state's chamber of commerce.

Finally, if you are buying wholesale and then reselling, you need a resale number in order to pay sales tax.

Outside Support and Self-Study Resources

The resources listed below provide a good start for figuring out all the technicalities of what you need to get your business going—and to stay out of trouble with the IRS, your state and local government, and the court system.

> *Your local public library.* Browse its website and visit the library in person to chat with a reference librarian.
>
> *Your local and state chambers of commerce.* Visit their websites to see what resources are available for members or the general public.
>
> *SCORE.* SCORE (www.score.org) offers free one-on-one mentoring on business topics as well as workshops, online tools, and more.
>
> *The SBA.* The U.S. Small Business Administration website (www.sba.gov) contains comprehensive, detailed information on every aspect of starting and running a small business, with links to other resources including state-specific regulations and processes. See this book's appendix for a sampling.
>
> *Publications.* See especially *Working for Yourself: Everything the Self-Employed Need to Know about Taxes, Recordkeeping, and Other Laws,* by Beth Williams and Dr. Jean Murray (Ocala, FL: Atlantic, 2008).

Following the basic recommendations and resources listed in this chapter will put your home-based business start-up on a secure footing. With the next chapter, we consider the practicalities of creating a functional office within your home.

Note

1. The Small Business Administration provides a handy list of each state's process at www.sba.gov/content/register-your-fictitious-or-doing-business-dba-name/.

SEVEN

Home Sweet Headquarters

Ideally, when you start a home-based business from scratch, you do so with open eyes, a firm grasp on the fundamentals covered in chapter 6, and flexible, creative decisions about the tangible and intangible setup of your new business. This chapter provides some areas to consider to help you make the very best decisions.

Your Work-from-Home Setup

It is difficult to know what your workspace should be like, or even what your daily work will be, when your at-home business is just an idea. But take a few minutes to picture yourself one year from now, when your start-up is successful and you are meeting your short-term goals. What do your workdays look like? What do you need to complete tasks efficiently? With that image of your future in mind, you can better estimate what size workspace you need, what type of you equipment you'll rely on, and other important factors.

The Bigger the Workspace, the Bigger the Deduction

If you have a large enough home to warrant a sizable workspace, consider spreading out a bit. Remember, the percentage of your home devoted exclusively to a home office is the percentage of your mortgage or rent, utility bills, and other expenses that you can deduct on your taxes.

Imagine, for example, that you have a 2,000-square-foot home with a 200-square-foot bedroom. If you dedicate that whole room to your self-employment, you will be able to deduct 10 percent (200/2,000) of these expenses from your taxes. If you use only half of the room for your work, the allowable deduction drops to 5 percent, and down to 2 or 3 percent if you use just a corner of the room. In any case, be careful—or understand the risks of stretching the point. Remember that the space you claim should be used exclusively for your work. Imagine showing an IRS auditor the laptop set up on an end table in a room that obviously is set up for sleeping, exercising on your stepper, and storing your clothes.

A final word on deducting office expenses: if you don't have enough room for your business's materials or merchandise, or prefer not to store everything at home, remember that any space you rent for your business is also tax-deductible.

Meeting-Space Dilemma

Will you have clients, prospects, vendors, or colleagues coming to your home regularly? If so, consider where you might meet with them. If possible, create a small meeting space in or near your workspace. Consider which entrance you want visitors to use and the area of your home they'll walk through to reach the work area. Is it safe (e.g., no hazardous stairs, toy-strewn rugs, or overprotective dogs)? Are you able to steer clear of other household members? Do you care if it makes you appear less than professional?

Occasionally customers come to Roslyn Broder's home to examine her RedAvaDesigns jewelry, for repairs, or to buy. "I don't have a problem with having someone come over as long as I've met the person and think they're okay."

If you don't want clients or prospects in your home—whether because of security concerns, to appear more professional, or to keep your clients free of dog hair—you should be able to find a reasonable alternative besides joining them in their car in your driveway. Check your public library to see if you can reserve a meeting room. Ask around. Maybe a friend or family member has an employer that might loan you an empty office or conference room for an hour—or, you can always rent temporary office space by the hour. For some situations a quiet coffee shop may do the trick.

Inventory and Upgrade Your Equipment

It's hard to think of any type of home-based business that wouldn't benefit from a computer—at least for record keeping and billing purposes. Most likely your desktop, laptop, or tablet will be the lifeline of what you do—and you don't have an employer to rely on to provide that lifeline. It's all up to you, so put on your IT/office manager hat:

Is your current computer adequate for your business? You need one that you don't have to share with others in your household, which ideally you can claim is for business use only (for the IRS), with enough memory and speed for what you plan to do.

How is your Internet connection? If it isn't speedy and 100 percent reliable, consider changing service providers or upgrading your service. Before you do, decide whether you need wireless Internet for your home so that you can roam as you work.

How secure is your system? Make sure you have a solid firewall against hackers, and set up a daily backup for your work files.

How dated is your software? If you'll be sharing files with customers, you should ensure that you are working with recent versions of the most common programs, such as Microsoft Office and Adobe Acrobat.

What will you do when you need to call tech support? Ask around *before* your computer crashes, and get some recommendations of vendors (including self-employed individuals) who make house calls.

Your business may call for investment in some computer peripherals, perhaps a good printer, scanner, or external hard drive. In these, as in all purchases for building your business, you walk a fine line between not spending more than you can afford and acquiring the tools you need to compete.

Along with your computer, your telephone is your connection to your customers, prospective customers, and the entire outside world. Before you pick up the phone, ask yourself:

Do I need a separate mobile phone or landline dedicated to my business? Perhaps one of your current phones can do double-duty, as long as you have a professional-sounding voicemail greeting and answer unknown calls in a businesslike manner.

If I'm using my home phone for my business, do I need caller ID? This lets you know instantly whether you're getting a call for your new business, a personal call, or a call from a telemarketer—and you can answer accordingly, or not at all.

How often am I going to be on the phone? If it's a lot of time, invest in a comfortable headset or earbuds, or a phone with speaker options. But use a speakerphone only if your home office is quiet.

Can I keep it charged? Mobile phones and cordless handsets tend to run out of battery power within a phone-call-filled day. Make sure you have a convenient plan in place for recharging during the day. A second handset for your landline is also a good idea.

Many home-based, self-employed people enjoy the freedom of being able to work from a coffee shop, or of sneaking out for a walk or a meal during the day. Others—such as those in the building trades, dog walkers, and home inspectors—are routinely out and about on business.

If you know that your business will be more "out of home" than "at home," take this into account when considering what equipment you need. Do your research on available communication tools, including tablet computers and smartphones, to determine what you need and whether you can forego a traditional computer in favor of one of these mobile devices. And don't forget, whether you are working at home or on the go, business expenses such as cell phone contracts are deductible—to the extent that you are using them for business.

Stake Out Security Issues

As you are setting up your home-based business and starting to think about letting prospective customers know where to find you, make safety a priority.

Protect Your Property

When you open a home-based business, a lot more people may become aware of you, from the delivery truck driver who now stops at your door regularly, to your customers, to the new colleagues you meet when networking for new business. If you are going to be out of town, be careful when alerting your customers or vendors. You may need to let some of them know that you'll be unavailable, but word that message carefully so that it doesn't sound as if your home will be empty: "I won't be in my office for a few days, but I can take care of your project starting Monday," rather than "My wife and I are going on vacation." This goes for everything from casual conversations to answering-machine messages and automatic out-of-office e-mail replies.

Protect Your Privacy

Before you establish your business identity (see below), consider what contact information you want to give out. Are you comfortable making your home address public? You might prefer to use a P.O. box address for all business communications—if you have to list a mailing address at all. And using your mobile phone number will make you less traceable than using a landline.

Protect Your Personal Information

Starting a business can increase your risk of identity theft. When you are a sole proprietor, it is normal for new customers to request your Social Security number for tax purposes—but it's up to you to find the most secure way to share that information. That way is not e-mail, which can be hacked. The best way is to give the number directly to your contact over the phone, or to fax it on the condition that your contact is waiting for the document to come through. Don't just fill out, sign, and fax a W-2 to a company without getting some assurance that only the right people will see it (and your Social Security number) when it gets there.

You also need to secure your computer against hackers, particularly if you keep confidential or financial information on your hard drive. Make sure you keep a secure firewall up-to-date, and password-protect your computer and any backup device.

Protect Your Clients

If your business involves handling sensitive client information, it is your ethical and legal obligation to protect that data. Suppose, for example, that you are an independent real estate agent. Your files contain forms with clients' names, Social Security numbers, and bank account numbers. If someone hacks your computer, burgles your home, or simply rifles through your files while you're in the other room, that person could use this sensitive information for fraud or identity theft.

If you collect information like this, you must follow any state and industry laws on how that information is protected and disposed of. For instance, the Federal Trade Commission's Disposal Rule requires businesses to adopt appropriate disposal practices to prevent the unauthorized access to—or use of—information in a consumer report. Be sure you check for applicable laws that dictate how you handle and dispose of personal information.

Your Business Identity

Just as you set up a home workspace for your new business, which may change as you get settled into self-employment, so too you set up an identity for your business. This identity sets the tone for how your customers and prospective customers see you; it can make your home-based business seem more professional and help set you apart from the competition.

Depending on your commitment, budget, and intentions for your business, you may choose to invest in not just a DBA name but a logo, a tagline, or even an entire marketing campaign to establish your identity. On the other end of the spectrum, you may simply start working under your own name and craft an elevator pitch and a few materials that show who you are and what you do. Either way, your business identity helps communicate that you are a businessperson, not just someone without a job who's home all day.

Perhaps you are an independent software consultant, contracting with a single agency for long-term projects. Even if you do not seek other work or market your business, your agency contacts get the message that you are professional by way of the "identity" that comes through in your e-mail content, address, and signature as well as the clean, consistent layout of your invoices and time sheets. The results put you in line for more work, ahead of other contractors who don't maximize these tools.

Here are some basic components of your business identity, which you should plan out from your early days:

> *Business name.* Are you going to work under your own name or create a company name? If you decide to name your business (see chapter 6), give the name careful consideration—this will be your first impression and your first sales tool.

Illusion of employees. Many freelancers or sole proprietors choose to imply that their business comprises more than one person: their websites tout what "we" can do for clients, and their business name may even include "and associates." Following this path gives your customers and prospects the idea that a team of professionals is available to work for them. Consider whether this could be a good thing, netting you some new business, or a bad thing, setting expectations too high.

Look and feel. Even if you don't have the type of business (or the type of budget) that invests in advertising, mass e-mail, professional letterhead, and other marketing and identity pieces, you can still create a professional look and feel for your business. You can trade services with a graphic designer in return for a logo and "branding package," or you can design your own identity. Choose one or two typefaces for all communications, and do the same with colors. Your choices should let your business's personality shine through: Is it serious and corporate? Fun and catchy? Modern and cutting-edge? Use your chosen elements consistently on any documents you create. Once you set your identity, stick to it. Create a signature for all outgoing e-mail that includes your business contact information. You can use colors and multiple fonts (sparingly), but avoid adding more than one graphic. Keep the same design elements with any and all marketing materials for your business, including mass e-mail, mailings, ads, brochures or flyers, and web banners. Your online presence may, depending on your business, include a website (even if it's just one page), a LinkedIn page (for you or for your business), or your business's Facebook page. You won't be able to apply your look and feel to other sites, but repeat certain phrases and sentences among these online pages to strengthen your identity. Anything you send to your customers and prospects, including invoices, receipts, forms and applications, and even thank-you notes, should be designed with the same look and feel.

Domain name: Your website identity. Your first step in creating a website for any business is selecting the domain name or address. Obviously, your choice of domain name is an integral part of your identity. Keep it short, memorable, and appropriate—ideally, simply your name or business name.

Because each domain name is unique, you may not get your first choice. You may find that your preferred domain name is already in use by someone else. You find out if a name is already taken when you register your domain online. Visit Register.com, Godaddy.com, or Networksolutions.com and type in your desired domain. If the domain has not already been purchased—and it may be, even if there is no current website up—you can register it for a year or longer for a fee. (The fees vary, so shop around for the best deal.) If, however, the domain name has already been registered, you'll have to try different variations on the name, or take a different direction in naming entirely, until you find an acceptable and available address for your website.

Once you have a domain name, consider using it for your e-mail address(es) as well. You might need some help with this, but you can redirect e-mail from your current address to a new address, though you'll have to keep your current address active.

Once you've got your home-based business up and running—from your home office to the look and feel of your communications—it's time to work on ensuring your success. Chapter 8 touches on some vital success factors for any type of business.

EIGHT

Running Your Home-Based Business

This chapter should give you enough of an overview of good business practices to get you headed down the right track. As with the tax, insurance, and legal information offered in chapter 6, you can easily find more resources for details on the areas you need to learn.

Start with a Business Plan

You may not have to show your plan to anyone or formalize it, but when you complete a business plan for your home-based endeavor you clarify what you'll be doing and how you'll be doing it. And that's important for keeping you on track and headed for success. Additionally, if you seek outside funding for your business, you do need a formal, perfect business plan to show to investors.

You can start with a sample business plan—visit www.sbdcnet
.org/small-business-information-center/business-plans for samples—and do some research and thinking as you tailor it to your
specific circumstance.[1] You'll develop some valuable insights into
what you're doing when you write the following plan elements:

> *Business description.* Concise overview of your business,
>   including what specific products or services you offer
> *Competitive analysis.* Overview of your direct competition,
>   including local, global, and virtual competitors, and how
>   each compares to your business
> *Marketing plan.* Brief but comprehensive outline of your
>   plan for getting clients or business
> *Accounting plan.* Accounting system you will use and why

The appendix of this book includes more detailed advice from the
Small Business Administration on putting together a sound business plan.

Your business plan is a working document, so don't let it gather
dust once your first draft is complete. Refer to it as you go about
your business, and plan to review and update it as needed every
six to twelve months

Brace Yourself for a Bumpy Start

Be prepared to take your income for a roller-coaster ride when you
run your own business. No matter how hard you work, how good
your reputation, or how much money you make one week, everything can change overnight. You have no control over many of the
factors that can torpedo your business, such as the twists and turns
of the global economy and your little market, changes with your
clients and prospects, or just plain luck. The amount of work you

get can rise and fall, and with it your monthly income. You may end up working a lot, but clients may be slow to pay.

> "I wish I had started out being careful with my personal expenses. Working independently, you have times when there is no work, so you must have funds for rainy days. I learned that lesson when there was not much work."
>
> —*Mauricio Gutierrez, senior airport planner/engineer*

The best way to prepare for this up-and-down income is to plan for the worst. Be frugal in spending when you set up your new home-based business, save enough to pay your taxes, and try to put away money for the slow periods.

When starting your business, consider ways to save money in the long-term *before* you're established. For instance, look at utilities and see how you might save some money. Do you really need a landline *and* a mobile phone for your business? The same may apply to your home phones.

If you're shopping around for savings on an Internet provider, switch your e-mail address immediately to a free web-based service like Gmail or Yahoo. No matter how often you change providers in the future, your e-mail address won't change—and if and when you get your own domain name you can "attach it" to a free address.

Depending on your situation and how much you rely on a vehicle, consider whether you need to keep a car if you're no longer commuting. Maybe your multicar family can make do with one fewer vehicle, or you can get by with renting a Zipcar or I-GO car as needed. If you make no other change, at least alert your auto insurance carrier that you are no longer commuting every day; your rate should be adjusted down.

Put off purchasing or upgrading equipment until you're certain a change is necessary. You may find that you rarely or never need a printer/copier/scanner, and that your old printer is all you use.

The good news is that you may be able to help regulate the unevenness of your income by controlling how you are paid. If you do regular work for the same client, work out an agreement in which you are paid weekly. If you land a big project, don't wait for a big check after you're done; arrange to be paid in installments throughout the project, including a percentage paid before you begin (see "Money Matters II" below).

Get the Word Out

No matter what type of business you start, you need to let potential clients know that it exists. Fortunately, getting the word out doesn't necessarily entail a full-scale marketing campaign or a super-sized budget. Your basic marketing plan (which should be included in your business plan) should answer the following questions:

Who is most likely to purchase my product or service? Supplement your experience and knowledge of your area with a little research and creative thinking.

How can I reach these prospects most effectively? If your target market is, for example, local physicians' offices, it should be simple to find all of them and identify the appropriate contact within each. If your market is households within driving distance that have dogs, consider how to reach them through local veterinary offices, pet stores, pet-related charities, signage, and media.

What is my main message or strongest selling point for this audience? To market effectively, highlight one or two aspects that set you apart from the competition. Are your rates lower? Do you offer a money-back guarantee on your services? Can you get client referrals that serve as glowing recommendations?

In addition to answering these questions and acting on your answers, you are likely to need some basic marketing tools to support your business, such as a dedicated website. If a prospective client hears about your business, she may search for more information on the Internet. Finding your business site—even if it is only one page—helps establish your trustworthiness and professionalism.

Another tool that all self-employed people should use is business cards. It is easy and inexpensive to create your own cards these days—so do it, and hand them out when networking (formally and informally), leave several with your clients, include them in mailings, drop them off at local businesses, and keep them on hand all the time.

Virtual Business Cards

Some clients and prospects may prefer getting a virtual business card from you. Each major smartphone has business card apps you can choose from, or you can use SMS text messages to send cards through services such as Contxts.com. But continue to use the old-fashioned paper business card as well. Anyone can receive your hard-copy card, regardless of their communications equipment, and finding it in their pocket or on their desk is more likely to bring you to mind later.

When developing marketing materials, from your print-it-yourself business card to a mass e-mail series, remember to use the business identity you decided on (see chapter 7).

Unless you are a graphic designer, you may find that you need some help in creating marketing materials. Yes, you can find software that lets you design and post your own website—but unless the result looks polished and professional, reinforces your identity, and is error-free, you may end up driving business away with your efforts. The trick is to understand when your own efforts may not be good enough. If you are unsure, ask a brutally honest friend or family member to critique your design efforts, writing, naming ability, or marketing know-how. And if you realize you need to call in a pro, there are different options to consider.

You may be able to agree to a fair trade of services with a professional designer, webmaster, or writer. A self-employed massage therapist, for example, might trade massages for design and copywriting to get his initial marketing materials created.

Call in favors. Perhaps you loaned your brother-in-law the creative director money last year when he was out of work. Now it's time for him to pay the "interest." If you do call in a favor, keep it professional. Agree to a reasonable amount of work with a set deadline, and put it in writing (an e-mail will do).

You might also hire a student and save money. Many young people are learning digital design these days.

Addressing the Work-from-Home Angle

When you are putting your marketing in place and working with your business identity, you may need to address the fact that you are a self-employed individual working from home. Fortunately, in today's business world this is a common scenario that your clients should be comfortable with. But there are issues you should be prepared to address:

Confidentiality/security. If your work incorporates dealing with confidential information, whether it is taking credit card numbers over the phone or creating a top-secret document for the launch of a new IPO, you should make security part of your marketing message. Mention that you are security-conscious in your marketing message, and consider incorporating details of your security process or approach on a separate page of your website. Prospects may need to know that your home computer setup has the same level of protection as a corporation's, and that you follow appropriate protocols even if you are not overseen by a director of operations.

Reliability. Some companies and individuals are still skittish about committing their business to an individual—especially one who doesn't even have a "real" office. What if you disappear in the middle of a project? How do they know you are reliable? Here are a few effective ways to show that you are here (at home) to stay:

Tesimonials. Share testimonials from current and previous clients on your website, on your LinkedIn page, or as a one-sheet printout you deliver to prospects. Solicit a testimonial (and specific permission to use it, with the person's name and title) as soon as you deliver work successfully, and keep accumulating them.

Samples. Demonstrate specific work you've accomplished. You can do this by showing actual samples if applicable (in person or on your website) or by writing up a case study that reads like a success story.

Materials. Use marketing materials that look permanent and polished rather than printing one-off flyers on your ink-jet printer.

Availability. If a prospective client (such as a past employer or current acquaintance) knows that you are working from home while keeping an eye on your children or aging parents, he may have reservations about your availability and focus. First, you need to ensure that you are truly available for work, even if it means establishing limited hours when you are available for meetings, phone calls, or online communications. Be realistic when figuring this out, and when you have a plan communicate that to these prospects: "I will be able to complete your project by the deadline but can guarantee to be available for discussions only on Tuesdays and Wednesdays. Otherwise, we can communicate by e-mail."

Drumming Up New Clients

Unfortunately, there is more to acquiring paying clients than implementing a marketing strategy and printing up business cards. You need to go out and find business proactively. If you are basing your new home-based business on work you've already done, you should have a built-in network to start with. If you're starting in a new field, you are likely to have some contacts who might be able to help, or even hire you.

Your first step should be to list everyone in your various address books who falls within the target market you've selected, as well as anyone you think is connected to that target market. Contact those people by phone, individual e-mail (not via an impersonal group message), with a personal letter or note, or in person to let each know about your new home-based business—and directly ask for their business or their help in networking.

Other ways to get new business are to broaden your network through professional associations (online and in person) and your local chamber of commerce, promote yourself through speaking engagements to appropriate groups, cold-call businesses or individuals (by e-mail or telephone), and ask clients and colleagues to introduce you to likely prospects.

You may be able to skip these steps by working exclusively through temp or employment agencies, which find the work for you. The trade-off is that the agency takes a hefty cut of the pay, leaving you with a substantially lower hourly rate than you would get on your own. But this might be worth it to you—less money but no time and effort spent marketing or searching for work.

Money Matters I: Keeping the Books

When you start your business, you'll need a bookkeeping or accounting system that, at the very least, allows you to keep track of money you owe and are owed, and it may do a lot more.

You don't need a CPA to handle the finances for your home-based business: The easiest way to track expenses and income is to set up a business checking account. Deposit all your business income into this account, and use your checks to pay all business expenses. To pay yourself, write yourself a check from this account, and cash the check or deposit it in your personal account. Seem like too much trouble? Keep in mind that separate accounts help prove to the IRS, and to your clients, that you are a sole proprietor and not an employee of your client or someone with a home-based hobby masquerading as a businessperson. If you keep separate accounts and are audited, you'll realize that the extra trouble of maintaining separate accounts was well worth it. If you don't keep separate accounts and are turned down by a corporation that doesn't want to risk its own audit over your employment status, you learn the same lesson the hard way.

Tracking Expenses and Income

In addition to your checking account register or online records, you should maintain records of your business income and expenses. This allows you to see at a glance what you're spending on and how much you're making, and it makes tax preparation a lot easier. Depending on the size of your business and your own preferences, you can do this manually, create a spreadsheet using Excel or shareware, or use a software program such as Quicken or QuickBooks. A software program can also be used to track payments and create invoices, create profit and loss statements, and import your information into tax preparation software.

Note that for tax purposes you need supporting documentation for your expense and income entries. You can't simply claim that you purchased a new printer/scanner for $300 last fall; you need a credit card receipt or cancelled check.

Which Accounting Method Is for You?

Your business can operate on one of two accounting methods: cash basis or accrual basis. The cash basis method is used by most small businesses that don't have an inventory of goods or offer credit. It simply means that you haven't earned income until the money is in your hands—or bank account, if you prefer. Likewise, you don't technically pay an expense until your money changes hands.

In the accrual basis method, you report income when it is actually earned (not collected) and expenses when they are incurred (not paid). Why would you use the accrual basis method? Well, some businesses are required to by the IRS. Specifically, any business that sells, produces, or purchases merchandise and keeps an inventory—but only if your profits exceed $1 million per year for three years in a row.

Money Matters II: How Do You Know the Price Is Right?

The price or rate you decide to charge is crucial to your business. Charge too much, and you'll have a hard time getting off the ground. Charge too little, and clients will perceive that you are not a valuable commodity—and you may not be able to earn a living. But how do you know how much is "just right"?

The pay rate for a self-employed professional is higher than that for a comparable employed person—sometimes a *lot* higher. Your pay must cover your costs of doing business, which include your health insurance, retirement savings, and vacation and sick time. It also covers the hours you work that are not billable, such as marketing your business and administrative tasks.

There are several resources you can turn to that help determine the "going rate" for your specific service or product, and I recommend that you use all of them:

> *Check all applicable professional associations.* Many
> publish average charges, salary information, and other
> financial details from their members. You may have to
> join an association to access this data, so try to determine
> if it is up-to-date and accurate before you shell out any
> membership dues.

Ask colleagues. Others in your business are curious to know "the state of rates," and some are willing to share what they charge. Just be sure to return the favor and let them know what you're asking or planning to ask for.

Be a mystery shopper. You don't have to pretend you are going to buy something; scope out what others are asking for similar products or services. You can do this in person (if your business is represented in retail, for example) or online. But when you are browsing the Internet, take prices for professional services with a grain of salt.

If you are pricing products, you should be able to set a rate based on mystery shopping. But make sure you are covering all your costs for materials and overhead and still making a profit. If you are hand-knitting scarves, for example, it is obvious that you won't be able to match the prices of mass-produced scarves found in Target stores.

If you are setting your rate for a service, that rate may be an hourly rate, a flat fee, or a retainer. (A retainer is a minimum amount charged up front on a regular basis, such as monthly.) Your field may dictate that you use only one of these, and clients may be wary or reluctant of the others. Use the rate resources recommended above to verify how businesses like yours typically charge, and follow suit.

For a larger project or a brand-new client, consider requesting an immediate payment of 20–50 percent upon agreement or contract, along with the costs of materials if applicable. This is generally an acceptable business practice and one that is strongly recommended if are working for a new client or one who is not local. (You would find it difficult to track down money owed from a long-distance client.)

"Price is a huge issue. I look at what other people are selling and for how much, both online and in person. I've also looked at the pricing formulas that crafters' websites offer, which calculate based on your costs of materials, time to make the item, time to sell the item, overhead, and profit. But I kind of know what people are willing to pay."

—*Roslyn Broder, owner of RedAvaDesigns jewelry business*

Money Matters III: Bill It and Collect It

When it comes time to send an invoice for your work, don't be shy and don't procrastinate. Send your bill promptly, be polite and professional, and keep track of when payment is due to ensure that you're paid on time.

If your clients are businesses, it is nearly always acceptable to e-mail an invoice as a PDF. This is a quick and reliable delivery method that is usually preferred by recipients.

Include standard payment terms on all invoices you send out. This includes the time frame in which you expect to be paid, such as "net due 15 days" or "payable upon receipt." This should be the shortest amount of time you think is reasonable for clients to pay; a large corporation may have standards requiring thirty or sixty days to process an invoice, but the neighbor who hired you to install a ceiling fan should be able to pay immediately. Your payment terms may also include information on late fees, or, if you like, the discount for paying immediately.

In addition to a date, each invoice should include a unique identifying number that you can refer to if a problem arises. This is especially important when you are billing the same client similar amounts; it helps both parties track which invoices have been paid. Create your own numbering system and save copies of all outstanding invoices so that you can refer to that number when asking for payment.

Note that you may be asked to provide your Social Security number with your first invoice to a client. This is for tax purposes and is a legitimate request, but that doesn't mean you have to share your information with everyone indiscriminately. Ask if you can give the number directly to the correct contact in the accounting department over the phone.

Use a reliable system to log the date an invoice goes out and when you are paid. If a payment is overdue, follow up immediately. Often invoices haven't been forwarded for payment, and a nudge from you will get the ball rolling again. This is as simple as resending the invoice to your client with a note asking for a status update on your payment.

When it comes to payment, you will of course accept checks or direct deposits from your clients. But what about other payment methods? If you want to offer the convenience of taking credit cards, you need to set up a merchant account first. You can do this through your bank, but note that there are fees involved both for the initial setup and for processing transactions. Alternatively, consider using a PayPal account tied to your business bank account; it is easy to set up, clients can pay online securely, and deposits appear in your account within a day or two.

Collecting Your Money

It is shockingly common for self-employed professionals to have difficulty getting paid for their work. According to the nonprofit Freelancers Union website, three out of four freelancers are paid late or not paid at all at least once in their careers.[2] Here are some steps to take, beginning within two weeks of a missed payment date:

▸ If you are being paid in stages or installments, stop work as soon as a payment is late, and don't restart until you are paid per your agreement.

▸ If your client does not respond to your second-notice invoice, follow up with a phone call, confirming the client's receipt of the bill and asking about the payment status.

▸ If there is no response to repeated attempts to contact your client, or you are told point-blank that the client cannot or will not pay you, it is necessary to escalate your collection efforts.

▸ Be persistent and don't let a week go by that you are not in contact with someone. After a few attempts with your client contact, ask to communicate directly with an individual in the accounting department. In all calls and e-mail messages, be professional and firm.

▸ Keep a written log of each attempt to get payment, including a summary of phone conversations. You may need to refer to this if you end up in court.

▸ If repeated attempts do not result in payment, mail a final demand letter to your client contact. This brief letter should state how much is owed, when it was due, and what action you are taking if you do not receive payment by a specific date. You may want to hire an attorney to write and send this letter; your increased chances of getting payment may be worth the cost.

If during this process your client requests special payment terms, such as paying off the total with a weekly or biweekly partial payment, it is worth considering. If the offer is genuine, you are much

more likely to collect at least some of the money owed. If you do
agree to a payment plan, put the terms in writing.

Your last resort for trying to wring your money out of a deadbeat
client is to go to court or hire a collection agency. Either way, you
are not likely to get any more work out of that client. And note that
each option, reviewed below, for pursuing your money to the bitter
end has limitations:

> *Small claims court.* Depending on your state legal system,
> your small claims court will handle disputes involving
> between $2,000 and $15,000. Larger claims can be sued
> in superior court. You don't need to hire an attorney to
> take someone to small claims court, and in fact some
> states don't allow attorneys. The problem with small
> claims court is that you can win the case and the court
> may order the client to pay you either the full amount
> owed or part of it, but the court won't enforce that
> payment. If your client won't pay the court judgment
> amount, you have to continue to work to get your money.
> In this case, you can hire an attorney and file a lien on
> the client's property, tap the client's bank account, or
> seize personal or business property. Remember, if you
> are dealing with an LLC or corporation, you will go
> after company assets; if your client is a sole proprietor or
> general partnership, you can go after personal assets.
>
> *Arbitration.* In arbitration, you and your client pay an
> arbitrator, or private mediator, who decides the case
> and files it with the court. The same results as with
> small claims court apply, and you may need to continue
> chasing your money.
>
> *Collections.* You can hire a collection agency to get the
> money for you. However, if you have only one debt to

collect, it must be a substantial amount or you won't find an agency that will take the job. Still, you *can* pay a collection agency a fee to write multiple collection letters to your clients. Otherwise, you don't pay a collection agency directly. Rather, they take a percentage of the money they collect for you—anywhere from 15 to 50 percent, depending on how large the debt is, among other factors. Get an agreement in writing in advance. If you do want to pursue this avenue, ask around for a personal referral of an agency and then check them out with the Better Business Bureau and online.

Check Them Out

Unfortunately, if a legally protected organization goes out of business or disappears without paying you, none of the options listed above will work. That's why it is important to do some research on any new client and try to get some payment in advance for your work.

If you are concerned about not getting paid by a new client, you can do some legwork yourself to check the prospective client out. The easiest way to is to run a credit check on a business through an organization like Dun & Bradstreet. You pay a fee each time you do it, but you can request a report online at http://smallbusiness .dnb.com and get it within a day. You can find out if a company is a habitual late payer or nonpayer, or if it is currently embroiled in a lawsuit or bankruptcy proceeding.

Alternatively, you can request credit information and references from the client and check them yourself. It is common business practice to call each reference's accounting department and ask if they have had any payment problems with your prospective client. Be wary of false references, though. You can also see if there are any complaints against the company filed with the Better Business Bureau and perform a general Internet search to see what turns up. Finally, verify the form of ownership of any small companies you do work for to see whether an individual or a corporation would be liable for debts incurred.

Get It in Writing

A proven way to help protect yourself is to start every project or relationship with a written agreement. This may be a legally binding contract, a letter of agreement that is signed by both parties, or simply an e-mail that covers the basics of the agreement between you and the client regarding work and payment. Not only will a written agreement strengthen your case for getting paid, it clarifies the terms of the project before you begin, including time frame, your responsibilities, any limits to your work, and price.

An added benefit of working under a written agreement: it helps prove to the IRS that you are an independent contractor rather than an employee.

If the client provides you with a contract, read it over carefully and look for the following:

▸ A noncompete clause that prevents you from doing any work for another organization in the same field.
▸ A liability statement that shifts any lawsuit involving the work to you rather than to the corporation issuing the contract.
▸ A scope of project that is larger than you expected. If the contract appears to give you more responsibility or work, is your fee still reasonable, or should it be increased as well?

▸ Payment terms that are unfair or may present problems to you. For example, watch for promise of payment upon final approval of the work. What happens if you complete the assignment but it is never officially approved?

Ideally, you will create your own written agreements. This gives you control over the terms of work rather than having you accept a standard contract provided by a client. You can find an appropriate contract template to start from online and draft your own agreement letter. Once you have a complete draft, you can customize it for each client or project. Include spaces for you and a client representative to sign and date the letter, and keep a signed copy. Your agreement should cover, at minimum:

▸ A brief but comprehensive description of the work to be performed. If you are not precise, you could end up doing more than you planned, without compensation. For example, a graphic designer should specify the number of revisions she will make on a project and note that any additional revisions will be billed separately.

▸ A list of items, materials, or information the client is to provide to you so that you can do the work.

▸ A general time frame in which the work is to be completed. This may be for the client's benefit; keep it general or note the final deadline.

▸ Payment terms including when each payment is due. Any final payment should be required "upon completion," as noted earlier.

▸ Deadline for signing. Imagine sending an agreement letter to a new client in late August, eager for a lucrative project that will keep you busy all autumn. But then you don't get the final, signed letter back until December 15—and you no longer have the time to complete the project in the stated time frame. This is just one reason why you should end your letter with a warning that the terms outlined are only available for a limited time—say, two weeks or a month.

One last word on contracts and agreements: They are not set in stone. You or your client may choose to terminate the agreement at any time, as long as there is a justifiable reason. If, for example, you don't receive the initial payment as outlined, you should stop work. And if you don't deliver work when promised, your client can terminate the agreement.

Create Your Paper Trail

Contracts and agreements are just the tip of the iceberg when it comes to saving and filing records of your projects, your business, and your self-employment status. Make sure you have room for the following paper files:

Official forms. These include those documenting your incorporation, your DBA business name, and the like.

Insurance information. Know where to find this quickly in case you need to make a claim. Review your policy every year or two to see if you can reduce costs or need additional coverage.

Tax forms and supporting documentation. You need this if you're audited. You may also need these records for other reasons, such as proving income when applying for a mortgage.

Client files. Save copies of signed agreements and other communications for as long as you can. You may have reason to go back and check something for another project, or you may need to prove that you were working under contract for the client.

For those files that you keep electronically, make sure you have a reliable backup system—preferably one that backs up files to an off-site location (including the Internet).

Growing Your Business

If you are lucky and savvy enough to grow your business to the point that you need more people or room to be able to meet demand, tread carefully. Remember that a roller-coaster ride, with its sudden drops in income, can still be in your future. Don't grow so fast or so large that you won't be able to sustain your business in a downturn. Stay conservative when making decisions to expand.

Need Workers?

▶ *Don't* hire employees. The paperwork, legalities, insurance, and income tax that come with having employees is overwhelming for a one-person business.

▶ *Do* hire independent contractors as needed. Not only will you skip the headaches of becoming an employer, your workforce can ebb and flow to meet shifting demand. Ask around for recommendations, and have a stable of good "help" waiting when you need someone, or many someones.

▸ *Do* consider finding a business partner. If you partner with a professional similar to yourself, you can split the work—and because you established the business you should negotiate to receive a larger share of the profits.

Need More Room?

▸ *Don't* buy a larger home or office space. Unless your business is real estate, this is not a good way to invest your business income.

▸ *Do* consider renting space in a shared office. This is a flexible arrangement that can include administrative help, meeting space, equipment, and other factors that may suit your growing business.

▸ *Do* get creative in finding more room in your home. Remember, a larger work area translates to a larger deduction for many home office expenses. It may pay to put some money into insulating an attic or even rent a storage locker if it allows you to expand.

Need Administrative Help?

▸ *Don't* hire employees. (See above.)

▸ *Do* consider a virtual assistant. Depending on your agreement, you can use an assistant as much or as little as needed. You can hand over tasks you would give a secretary or intern or more skilled tasks such as social media posting, research, and even client calls.

▷ *Do* hire contractors to handle tasks such as your accounting, billing, and taxes; marketing the business; even sales to bring in new clients. This allows you to devote more time to the income-producing work.

Calling It Quits

Rather than taking your home-based business to the next level, you may decide that it is better to call it quits. Self-employed people move back to regular employment for a variety of reasons. Maybe you don't enjoy working for yourself after all, or you aren't able to generate enough income to cover your expenses (or make a living), or you simply miss the security and substantial benefits of full-time employment.

Whatever your reasons for putting your business to bed, do the right thing by your clients and others who may depend on you. Decide on a date when you'll officially stop doing business, and send out an announcement e-mail to everyone who should know, including current and past clients, your prospect list, vendors, and colleagues. Also post an announcement on your business website, LinkedIn page, or Facebook page and leave it up for at least three months. Eventually, take the pages down permanently.

If you can recommend a competitor (small business or sole proprietor) to fill your place with clients, do so—but talk to the competitor first.

You can let any business licenses, incorporation status, and the like expire without taking action.

We hope you can use the information in this chapter as a starting point, or an idea generator. Not all of the information here will apply to your specific home-based business, but you should pay attention to the sections that do. A business plan, solid and continual marketing, and money management are integral building blocks for a successful small business. If you find that you enjoy running a business from your home, you'll need to focus on these areas to ensure that you maintain that lifestyle.

Good luck!

Notes

1. The SBA also offers a template, "Guide for Writing a Business Plan," at www.sba.gov/content/templates-writing-business-plan/.
2. See "Get Paid, Not Played," Freelancers Union, www.freelancers union.org/resources/unpaidwages.html.

Small Business Administration Resources for Starting and Running a Small Business

20 Questions to Ask Yourself before Starting a Business

Many people dream of having their own business. To see if starting a business is right for you, ask yourself these important 20 questions. Your answers will help you determine if you are ready to become a small business owner or where you need to spend more time in planning.

1. Am I prepared to spend the time, money, and resources needed to get my business started?
2. What kind of business do I want?
3. What products/services will my business provide?
4. Why am I starting a business?
5. What is my target market?
6. Who is my competition?
7. What is unique about my business idea and the products/services I will provide?
8. How soon will it take before my products/services are available?
9. How much money do I need to get my business set up?
10. How long can I have to finance the company until I start making a profit?
11. Will I need to get a loan?
12. How will I price my product compared to my competition?
13. How will I market my business?
14. How will I set up the legal structure of my business?
15. How will I manage my business?
16. Where will I house my business?
17. How many employees will I need to start up?

18. What types of suppliers do I need to contact?
19. What kind of insurance do I need to invest in?
20. What do I need to do to ensure I am paying my taxes correctly?

Source: www.sba.gov/content/20-questions-before-starting-business

Do Your Market Research

To run a successful business, you need to learn all about your existing and potential customers, your competitors, and the economic conditions of your marketplace. Market research is the process of gathering and analyzing consumer and economic data to help you understand which products and services your customers want and how to differentiate your business from your competitors. Market research can also provide valuable insight to help you to:

▸ Reduce business risks
▸ Spot current and upcoming problems in the current market
▸ Identify sales opportunities
▸ Develop plans of action

How to Conduct Market Research

It's often difficult to know where to begin when making decisions about a business. A little planning can go a long way, so your first step should be to learn more about how to conduct market research. This article from AllBusiness.com provides basic information on how to conduct market research as well as related articles that can be helpful for you to make informed decisions about starting, growing, and managing your business: "Understanding the Basics of Small Business Research," www.allbusiness.com/marketing/market-research/2587-1.html.

Sources for Market Research Data

The federal government collects a wealth of data and information about businesses, industries, and economic conditions that can aid in conducting market research. The following sources for market data can provide starting points for learning more about your customers and competitors.

Business Data and Statistics

These statistical sources are often used for secondary market research. *Secondary research* is the most widely used method of collecting data and involves summarizing or synthesizing existing research from sources such as books, magazine articles, white papers, websites, etc.

  ▶ Consumer Statistics: www.marketresearch.com/
    Marketing-Market-Research-c70/Demographics-c81/
  ▶ Economic Indicators: www.esa.doc.gov/about
    -economic-indicators
  ▶ Employment Statistics: www.bls.gov
  ▶ Income and Earnings: www.bls.gov

International Markets

Are you interested in taking your business global? These resources will help you to research potential international markets for your products or services.

> ‣ Market Research Guide for Exporters (http://export
> .gov/mrktresearch/)
> Identifies resources for business owners seeking to
> sell their products abroad.
> ‣ Country Market Research (http://tcc.export.gov/
> Country_Market_Research/index.asp)
> Reports on trade issues in countries across the globe.
> ‣ BuyUSA.gov
> Helps U.S. companies find new international business
> partners in worldwide markets.

Green Business Markets

Being "green" isn't just a good business practice. It's a multi-billion-dollar industry. These resources will help you learn about marketing to environmentally conscious consumers.

> ‣ Environmental E-Market Express (http://export.gov/)
> Provides current environmental market research data,
> international trade leads and events.
> ‣ Talk the Walk (www.talkthewalk.net)
> Offers research and statistics on consumers'
> attitudes and behaviors in the context of successful
> green products and sustainable lifestyle marketing
> strategies.
> ‣ Green Consumers: A Growing Market for Local
> Businesses (www.uwex.edu/CES/cced/downtowns/
> ltb/lets/LTB1106.pdf)
> Explains how local businesses can better serve
> environmentally conscious consumers.
> ‣ Consumer Reports: Greener Choices (www.greener
> choices.org/eco-labels/eco-home.cfm?redirect=1)

Provides information on buying greener products that have minimal environmental impact and also meet personal needs.

Source: www.sba.gov/content/conducting-market-research

Essential Elements of a Good Business Plan

What are the key elements of a business plan? From market analysis to your company financials, this guide walks you through the essential components of your plan, including how to develop a funding request.

Business Plan Executive Summary

Your executive summary is a snapshot of your business plan as a whole and touches on your company profile and goals. The executive summary is often considered the most important section of a business plan. This section briefly tells your reader where your company is, where you want to take it, and why your business idea will be successful. If you are seeking financing, the executive summary is also your first opportunity to grab a potential investor's interest.

The executive summary should highlight the strengths of your overall plan and therefore be the last section you write. However, it usually appears first in your business plan document.

Below are several key points that your executive summary should include based on the stage of your business.

If You Are an Established Business

If you are an established business, be sure to include the following information:

> ▸ *The mission statement.* This explains what your business is all about. It should be between several sentences and a paragraph.

> ▸ *Company information.* Include a short statement that covers when your business was formed, the names of the founders and their roles, your number of employees, and your business location(s).

> ▸ *Growth highlights.* Include examples of company growth, such as financial or market highlights (for example, "XYZ Firm increased profit margins and market share year-over-year since its foundation"). Graphs and charts can be helpful in this section.

> ▸ *Your products/services.* Briefly describe the products or services you provide.

> ▸ *Financial information.* If you are seeking financing, include any information about your current bank and investors.

> ▸ *Summarize future plans.* Explain where you would like to take your business.

With the exception of the mission statement, all of the information in the executive summary should be covered in a concise fashion and kept to one page. The executive summary is the first part of your business plan many people will see: therefore, each word should count.

If You Are a Start-up or New Business

If you are just starting a business, you won't have as much information as an established company. Instead, focus on your experience and background as well as the decisions that led you to start this particular enterprise.

Demonstrate that you have done thorough market analysis. Include information about a need or gap in your target market, and how your particular solutions can fill it. Convince the reader that you can succeed in your target market, then address your future plans.

Market Analysis

The market analysis section of your business plan should illustrate your industry and market knowledge as well as any of your research findings and conclusions. This section is usually presented after the executive summary and the table of contents.

Industry description and outlook. Describe your industry, including its current size and historic growth rate as well as other trends and characteristics (e.g., life cycle stage, projected growth rate). Next, list the major customer groups within your industry.

Information about your target market. Narrow your target market to a manageable size. Many businesses make the mistake of trying to appeal to too many target markets.

Distinguishing characteristics. What are the critical needs of your potential customers? Are those needs being met? What are the demographics of the group, and where are they located? Are there any seasonal or cyclical purchasing trends that may impact your business?

Size of the primary target market. In addition to the size of your market, what data can you include about the annual purchases your market makes in your industry? What is the forecasted market growth for this group?

How much market share can you gain? What is the market share percentage and number of customers you expect to obtain in a defined geographic area? Explain the logic behind your calculation.

Pricing and gross margin targets. Define your pricing structure, gross margin levels, and any discount that you plan to use. When you include information about any of the market tests or research studies you have completed, be sure to focus only on the results of these tests. Any other details should be included in the appendix.

Competitive Analysis. Your competitive analysis should identify your competition by product line or service and market segment. Assess the following characteristics of the competitive landscape:

- Market share
- Strengths and weaknesses
- How important is your target market to your competitors?
- Are there any barriers that may hinder you as you enter the market?
- What is your window of opportunity to enter the market?
- Are there any indirect or secondary competitors who may impact your success?
- What barriers to market are there (e.g., changing technology, high investment cost, lack of quality personnel)?

Regulatory restrictions. Include any customer or governmental regulatory requirements affecting your business, and how you'll comply. Also, cite any operational or cost impact the compliance process will have on your business.

Company Description

What do you do? What differentiates your business? Which markets do you serve?

This section of your business plan provides a high-level review of the different elements of your business. This is akin to an extended elevator pitch and can help readers and potential investors quickly understand the goal of your business and its unique proposition.

> ▸ Describe the nature of your business and list the marketplace needs that you are trying to satisfy.
> ▸ Explain how your products and services meet these needs.
> ▸ List the specific consumers, organizations, or businesses that your company serves or will serve.
> ▸ Explain the competitive advantages that you believe will make your business a success, such as your location, expert personnel, efficient operations, or ability to bring value to your customers.

Organization & Management

All businesses are structured differently. Describe your organization and its management structure.

Who does what in your business? What is their background, and why are you bringing them into the business as board members or employees? What are they responsible for? These may seem like unnecessary questions to answer in a one- or two-person organization, but the people reading your business plan want to know who's in charge, so tell them. Give a detailed description of each division or department and its function.

This section should include who's on the board (if you have an advisory board) and how you intend to keep them there. What kind of salary and benefits package do you have for your people? What incentives are you offering? How about promotions? Reassure your reader that the people you have on staff are more than just names on a letterhead.

Organizational Structure

A simple but effective way to lay out the structure of your company is to create an organizational chart with a narrative description. This will prove that you're leaving nothing to chance, you've thought out exactly who is doing what, and there is someone in charge of every function of your company. Nothing will fall through the cracks, and nothing will be done three or four times over. To a potential investor or employee, that is very important.

Ownership Information

This section should also include the legal structure of your business along with the subsequent ownership information it relates to. Have you incorporated your business? If so, is it a C or S corporation? Or perhaps you have formed a partnership with someone. If so, is it a general or limited partnership? Or maybe you are a sole proprietor.

Important ownership information that should be incorporated into your business plan includes:

- Names of owners
- Percentage ownership
- Extent of involvement with the company
- Forms of ownership (i.e., common stock, preferred stock, general partner, limited partner)
- Outstanding equity equivalents (i.e., options, warrants, convertible debt)
- Common stock (i.e., authorized or issued)

Management Profiles

Experts agree that one of the strongest factors for success in any growth company is the ability and track record of its owner/management team, so let your reader know about the key people in your company and their backgrounds. Provide résumés that include the following information:

- Name
- Position (include brief position description along with primary duties)
- Primary responsibilities and authority
- Education
- Unique experience and skills
- Prior employment
- Special skills
- Past track record
- Industry recognition
- Community involvement
- Number of years with company
- Compensation basis and levels (make sure these are reasonable—not too high or too low)

Be sure you quantify achievements (e.g., "Managed a sales force of ten people," "Managed a department of fifteen people," "Increased revenue by 15 percent in the first six months," "Expanded the retail outlets at the rate of two each year," "Improved the customer service as rated by our customers from a 60 percent to a 90 percent rating").

Also highlight how the people surrounding you complement your own skills. If you're just starting out, show how each person's unique experience will contribute to the success of your venture.

Board of Directors' Qualifications

The major benefit of an unpaid advisory board is that it can provide expertise that your company cannot otherwise afford. A list of well-known, successful business owners/managers can go a long way toward enhancing your company's credibility and perception of management expertise.

If you have a board of directors, be sure to gather the following information when developing the outline for your business plan:

- Names
- Positions on the board
- Extent of involvement with company
- Background
- Historical and future contribution to the company's success

Marketing & Sales Management

How do you plan to market your business? What is your sales strategy? In this section, the first thing you want to do is define your marketing strategy. There is no single way to approach a marketing strategy; your strategy should be part of an ongoing business-evaluation process and unique to your company. However, there are common steps you can follow which will help you think through the direction and tactics you would like to use to drive sales and sustain customer loyalty.

An overall marketing strategy should include four different strategies:

- A market penetration strategy.
- A growth strategy. This strategy for building your business might include: an internal strategy such as how to increase your human resources, an acquisition strategy such as buying another business, a franchise strategy for branching out, a horizontal strategy where you would provide the same type of products to different users, or a vertical strategy where you would continue providing the same products but would offer them at different levels of the distribution chain.
- Channels of distribution strategy. Choices for distribution channels could include original equipment manufacturers (OEMs), an internal sales force, distributors, or retailers.
- Communication strategy. How are you going to reach your customers? Usually a combination of the following tactics works the best: promotions, advertising, public relations, personal selling, and printed materials such as brochures, catalogs, flyers, etc.

After you have developed a comprehensive marketing strategy, you can then define your sales strategy. This covers how you plan to actually sell your product.

Your overall sales strategy should include two primary elements:

▷ *A sales force strategy.* If you are going to have a sales force, do you plan to use internal or independent representatives? How many salespeople will you recruit for your sales force? What type of recruitment strategies will you use? How will you train your sales force? What about compensation for your sales force?

▷ *Your sales activities.* When you are defining your sales strategy, it is important that you break it down into activities. For instance, you need to identify your prospects. Once you have made a list of your prospects, you need to prioritize the contacts, selecting the leads with the highest potential to buy first. Next, identify the number of sales calls you will make over a certain period of time. From there, you need to determine the average number of sales calls you will need to make per sale, the average dollar size per sale, and the average dollar size per vendor.

Service or Product Line

What do you sell? How does it benefit your customers? What is the product life cycle? Do you plan R&D activities? Tell the "story" of your product or service.

A Description of Your Product / Service
Include information about the specific benefits of your product or service—from your customers' perspective. You should also talk about your product or service's ability to meet consumer needs, any advantages your product has over that of the competition,

and the current development stage your product is in (e.g., idea, prototype).

Details about Your Product's Life Cycle

Be sure to include information about where your product or service is in its life cycle, as well as any factors that may influence its cycle in the future.

Intellectual Property

If you have any existing, pending, or anticipated copyright or patent filings, list them here. Also disclose whether any key aspects of a product may be classified as trade secrets. Last, include any information pertaining to existing legal agreements, such as non-disclosure or non-compete agreements.

Research and Development (R&D) Activities

Outline any R&D activities that you are involved in or are planning. What results of future R&D activities do you expect? Be sure to analyze the R&D efforts of not only your own business, but also of others in your industry.

Funding Request

If you are seeking funding for your business, include your current funding requirement, any future funding requirements over the next five years, explanation of how you intend to use the funds you receive, and any strategic financial situational plans for the future, such as a buyout or selling your business.

Financial Projections

If you need funding, providing financial projections to back up your request is critical. The financials should be developed after you've analyzed the market and set clear objectives. That's when you can allocate resources efficiently. The following is a list of the critical financial statements to include in your business plan packet.

Historical Financial Data

If you own an established business, you will be requested to supply historical data related to your company's performance. Most creditors request data for the last three to five years, depending on the length of time you have been in business.

The historical financial data you would want to include would be your company's income statements, balance sheets, and cash flow statements for each year you have been in business (usually for up to three to five years). Often creditors are also interested in any collateral that you may have that could be used to ensure your loan, regardless of the stage of your business.

Prospective Financial Data

All businesses, whether start-up or growing, will be required to supply prospective financial data. Most of the time, creditors will want to see what you expect your company to be able to do within the next five years. Each year's documents should include forecasted income statements, balance sheets, cash flow statements, and capital expenditure budgets. For the first year, you should supply monthly or quarterly projections. After that, you can stretch it to quarterly and/or yearly projections for years two through five.

Make sure that your projections match your funding requests; creditors will be on the lookout for inconsistencies. It's much better if you catch mistakes before they do. If you have made assumptions in your projections, be sure to summarize what you have assumed. This way, the reader will not be left guessing.

Finally, include a short analysis of your financial information. Include a ratio and trend analysis for all of your financial statements (both historical and prospective). Since pictures speak louder than words, you may want to add graphs of your trend analysis (especially if they are positive).

Appendix

An appendix is optional, but a useful place to include information such as résumés, permits, leases, and so on.

Source: www.sba.gov/category/navigation-structure/starting-managing
-business/starting-business/how-write-business-plan/e

Guide for Writing a Business Plan

What Goes into a Business Plan?

There is no single formula for developing a business plan, but some elements are consistent throughout all business plans. Your plan should include an executive summary, a description of the business, a plan for how you will market and manage your business, financial projections, and the appropriate supporting documents.

To help you get started in writing your business plan, we have summarized the essential elements in the following outline.

Elements of a Business Plan

1. Cover sheet
2. Executive summary (statement of the business purpose)
3. Table of contents
4. Body of the document

    A. Business

    1. Description of business
    2. Marketing
    3. Competition
    4. Operating procedures
    5. Personnel
    6. Business insurance

B. Financial data

    1. Loan applications
    2. Capital equipment and supply list
    3. Balance sheet
    4. Breakeven analysis
    5. Profit and loss statements
    6. Three-year summary
    7. Detail by month, first year
    8. Detail by quarters, second and third year
    9. Assumptions upon which projections were based
   10. Pro-forma cash flow

C. Supporting documents

    1. Tax returns of principals (partners in the business) for last three years, personal financial statements (all banks have these forms)
    2. Copy of franchise contract and all supporting documents provided by the franchisor (for franchise businesses)
    3. Copy of proposed lease or purchase agreement for building space
    4. Copy of licenses and other legal documents
    5. Copy of résumés of all principals
    6. Copies of letters of intent from suppliers, etc.

Source: www.sba.gov/content/templates-writing-business-plan

Finding a Niche: Make Your Business Plan Stand Out

One of the first steps to business planning is determining your target market and why they would want to buy from you.

For example, is the market you serve the best one for your product or service? Are the benefits of dealing with your business clear, and are they aligned with customer needs? If you are unsure about the answers to any of these questions, take a step back and revisit the foundation of your business plan.

The following tips can help you clarify what your business has to offer, identify the right target market for it, and build a niche for yourself.

Be Clear about What You Have to Offer

Ask yourself: beyond basic products or services, what are you really selling? Consider this example: your town probably has several restaurants all selling one fundamental product—food, but each is targeted at a different need or clientele.

One might be a drive-thru fast food restaurant, perhaps another sells pizza in a rustic Italian kitchen, and maybe there's a fine dining seafood restaurant that specializes in wood-grilled fare. All these restaurants sell meals, but they sell them to targeted clientele who are looking for the unique qualities each has to offer. What they are *really* selling is a combination of product, value, ambience, and brand experience.

When starting a business, be sure to understand what makes your business unique. What needs does your product or service fulfill? What benefits and differentiators will help your business stand out from the crowd?

Don't Become a Jack-of-All-Trades—Learn to Strategize

It's important to clearly define what you're selling. You do not want to become a jack-of-all trades and master of none because this can have a negative impact on business growth. As a smaller business, it's often a better strategy to divide your products or services into manageable market niches. Small operations can then offer specialized goods and services that are attractive to a specific group of prospective buyers.

Identify Your Niche

Creating a niche for your business is essential to success. Often, business owners can identify a niche based on their own market knowledge, but it can also be helpful to conduct a market survey with potential customers to uncover untapped needs. During your research process, identify the following:

- Which areas in which your competitors are already well-established
- Which areas are being ignored by your competitors
- Potential opportunities for your business

Source: www.sba.gov/content/finding-niche-make-your-business-plan-stand -out

Additional Web Resources

Association of Small Business Development Centers (ASBDC)
http://asbdc-us.org
Small-business owners, or anyone considering being one, can visit the ASBDC website to find helpful business resources or locate a Small Business Development Center in their area, where they can receive free business consulting.

Elance
www.elance.com
Elance is a virtual workplace that connects independent contractors with clients. Users can create a detailed profile of their services and apply for jobs posted by prospective clients.

FlexJobs
www.flexjobs.com
FlexJobs is a job search website for finding telecommuting and freelance jobs.

Freelancer.com
www.freelancer.com
Freelancers can offer their services, such as software development, writing, data entry, design, engineering, sales and marketing, and accounting, to prospective clients on Freelancer.com.

Freelancers Union
www.freelancersunion.org
A free membership with the Freelancers Union connects freelancers to group-rate benefits, resources, community, and other support.

Guidestar
www.guidestar.org
Guidestar is a free, searchable directory of nonprofit organizations.

Hoover's
www.hoovers.com
The Hoover's database includes detailed profiles of more than 65 million corporations and other organizations. Hoover's offers subscriptions and services for small businesses.

IRS Small Business and Self-Employed Tax Center
www.irs.gov/businesses/small/index.html
The Tax Center in the source for all things tax-related: find out how to obtain an EIN, download tax forms for independent contractors, and learn about healthcare tax provisions for the self-employed.

LinkedIn
www.linkedin.com
Setting up a free profile on LinkedIn connects you to jobs, prospects, networking opportunities, and business research.

Meetup
www.meetup.com
Browse Meetup to find some professional groups in your area or start your own, free-of-charge.

National Association for the Self-Employed (NASE)
www.nase.org
NASE offers resources and tools to run a successful business. A paid membership provides unlimited access to NASE consultants.

Occupational Outlook Handbook (OOH)
www.bls.gov/oco
Produced by the U.S. Bureau of Labor Statistics, the OOH provides free detailed career information for all types of occupations, information on state-by-state job markets, and job search tips.

oDesk
www.odesk.com
Independent contractors can use oDesk to find jobs in project management, customer support, marketing, design, web and software development, writing, translation, and legal services.

O*NET OnLine
www.onetonline.org
Sponsored by the U.S. Department of Labor and the Employment and Training Administration, O*NET OnLine is a database of nearly a thousand occupation profiles. Access to all information is free.

PayScale
www.payscale.com
According to its website, PayScale has collected "salary and career data from more than 35 million people, covering 12,000 unique job titles." Much of this content is free for users to access.

Salary.com
www.salary.com
Salary.com provides salary calculations and salary-related advice.

SCORE
www.score.org
SCORE is a nonprofit association dedicated to helping people start and grow small businesses. SCORE offers its services at no or very low cost.

U.S. Small Business Administration (SBA)
www.sba.gov
The SBA offers a variety of programs and support services to help people navigate the issues they face while starting and growing a small business. All information and tools on the website are free.

Telework Research Network
www.teleworkresearchnetwork.com
The Telework Research Network website is a good place to research trends in working from home.

Work at Home Jobs
www.workathomejobs.org
Work at Home is a job aggregator, free to use, that pulls in and lists many freelance jobs available online.

Working Home Guide
www.workinghomeguide.com
Online business owners and people who work online can visit Working Home Guide to read the latest news and information related to the online business industry.

WAHM.com (Work-at-Home Moms)
www.wahm.com
WAHM.com is a forum for work-at-home moms (and dads), who can browse its library of articles on home businesses and access work-at-home job boards.

Work at Home Careers
www.workathomecareers.com
Work at Home Careers is a work-at-home job search website.

Bibliography

Beshara, Tony. *Acing the Interview: How to Ask and Answer the Questions That Will Get You the Job.* New York: AMACOM, 2008.

Bolton, Robert, and Dorothy Grover Bolton. *People Styles at Work . . . and Beyond: Making Bad Relationships Good and Good Relationships Better.* 2nd ed. New York: AMACOM, 2009.

Carroll, Kevin, and Bob Elliott. *Make Your Point! Speak Clearly and Concisely Anyplace, Anytime.* Westport, CT: Second Avenue Press, 2009.

Directory of National Trade and Professional Associations. Bethesda, MD: Columbia Books, 2007.

Doyle, Alison. *Internet Your Way to a New Job: How to Really Find a Job Online.* 2nd ed. Cupertino, CA: Happy About, 2009.

Duffy, Marcia Passos. *Be Your Own Boss.* San Francisco: Wetfeet, 2006.

Fisher, Roger, and William L. Ury. *Getting to Yes: Negotiating Agreement without Giving In.* New York: Penguin, 1991.

Fishman, Stephen. *Working for Yourself: Law and Taxes for Independent Contractors, Freelancers, and Consultants.* Berkeley, CA: NOLO, 2011.

Hansen, Katharine. *A Foot in the Door: Networking Your Way into the Hidden Job Market.* Berkeley, CA: Ten Speed Press, 2008.

Ireland, Susan. *The Complete Idiot's Guide to the Perfect Resume.* 5th ed. New York: Alpha Books, 2010.

Jacoway, Kristen. *I'm in a Job Search—Now What??? Using LinkedIn, Facebook, and Twitter as Part of Your Job Search Strategy.* Cupertino, CA: Happy About, 2010.

Kanarek, Lisa. *Home Office Solutions: Creating a Space That Works for You.* Beverly, MA: Quarry Books, 2004.

Klaus, Peggy. *The Hard Truth about Soft Skills: Workplace Lessons Smart People Wish They'd Learned Sooner.* New York: HarperBusiness, 2007.

Levinson, Jay Conrad, and David E. Perry. *Guerrilla Marketing for Job Hunters 2.0: 1,001 Unconventional Tips, Tricks, and Tactics for Landing Your Dream Job.* Hoboken, NJ: John Wiley and Sons, 2009.

Oliver, Vicky. *301 Smart Answers to Tough Interview Questions.* Naperville, IL: Sourcebooks, 2005.

Pinkley, Robin L., and Gregory B. Northcraft. *Get Paid What You're Worth: The Expert Negotiators' Guide to Salary and Compensation.* New York: St. Martin's Griffin, 2003.

Price, Margaret. "Work at Home: Take Pay Cut. Come Out Ahead." *Christian Science Monitor,* July 25, 2011. www.csmonitor.com/business/2011/0725/work-at-home-take-pay-cut.-come-out-ahead.

Wall Street Journal Careers. "How to Write a Cover Letter." http://guides.wsj.com/careers/how-to-start-a-job-search/how-to-write-a-cover-letter/.

Warner, Ralph E. *Everybody's Guide to Small Claims Court.* Berkeley, CA: NOLO, 2010.

Whitwer, Glynnis. *Work @ Home: A Practical Guide for Women Who Want to Work from Home.* Birmingham, AL: New Hope Publishers, 2007.

Williams, Beth, and Dr. Jean Murray. *The Complete Guide to Working for Yourself: Everything the Self-Employed Need to Know about Taxes, Recordkeeping, and Other Laws.* Ocala, FL: Atlantic Publishing Group, 2008.

Yate, Martin. *Knock 'em Dead Cover Letters: Great Letter Techniques and Samples for Every Step of Your Search.* Avon, MA: Adams Media, 2008.

Index

Page numbers in italic refer to information in boxes.